The Process is full of wisdom in a world has allowed himself to be vulnerable at through crisis. I wish I had read this bo situations in my own life. It is deep, and in each stage of your walk with God.

– Cindy Jacobs
Generals International

For almost two decades I've watched Mattheus as he constantly seeks to encourage those around him to hear and act boldly on the promises in their lives. I have also seen him go through unbelievable storms. Because of these, I believe he has been forced to go deep into the heart of God, and he is stronger for everything he has worked through. His experience and reflection will reward readers as they seek to hold steady in their own course, following the promises of God through every season of life in Jesus.

– Heidi G. Baker, Ph.D.
Co-founder and executive chairman of the board, Iris Global

Our life in the Spirit is a process of claiming heaven's promises and making them real in our lives. Many of God's promises wait for us to grow, to mature, to reach out at the proper time, and claim them. I know that *The Process* is going to be underlined, studied and read a number of times by each one who gets this masterpiece!

– Dr Brian Simmons
The Passion Translation Project
Passion & Fire Ministries

Mattheus van der Steen's new book is a powerful and timely message. He shares from deeply personal experiences and rich biblical insight to help readers recognize the type of storm they are facing and to remain faithful to their calling. As Mattheus is a highly respected leader in the body of Christ, a fruitful evangelist and a dear personal friend, I wholeheartedly recommend *The Process*.

– Evangelist Daniel Kolenda
President, Christ for All Nations

The Process is an exceptional guide that offers practical and biblical insights to help readers fulfill their God-given purpose. With powerful stories and a structured approach, my dear friend Mattheus van der Steen provides a roadmap for transformation that is rooted in faith and grounded in God's Word. This book will inspire and empower readers to embrace the process of growth and change, and to trust God's plan for their lives.

– *Markus Wenz*
Director, Holy Spirit Night

The Process is a timely and much-needed truth that will guide the reader to move from the promise of their destiny to the fulfillment of that promise. I have known Mattheus for many years and have seen him "walk and practice" the biblical and life-giving principles he shared so clearly in this book. I totally recommend this book to anyone who desires strongly to live their life to the fullest.

– *Mel Tari*
Author 'Like A Mighty Wind'
President and founder, World Mission

In his newest book, *The Process*, Mattheus shares practical truth, revelation and life experience that has brought him through the process and into the fulfillment of God's promises. I was deeply moved and encouraged by the level of transparency and vulnerability that Mattheus shares. I know it will bless and encourage you, because Jesus is faithful in the process and always keeps His promises!

– *David Wagner*
Fathers Heart Ministries, Franklin, TN

One of my life verses is: "He wastes nothing, He gets me ready." It is my expression of Romans 8:28. As I have enjoyed my friendship with Mattheus, I have seen the way in which he has applied this to his life. The same character is on display in every season of the process ... Being with Mattheus always encourages me, gives me faith and inspires me for my own journey.

– *Paul Manwaring*
Senior leadership team, Bethel Church, Redding, CA

There is power in *The Process*! Those who have chosen to follow Jesus Christ for any length of time know that it is not only the power of His resurrection but also the fellowship of His sufferings that lead to maturity in the faith. Mattheus brings sensitive, real-life examples of the storms that we, as believers, may have to face, and also delivers practical ways to keep moving forward toward the finish line.

– Nathan Morris
Founder and president, Shake The Nations Ministries, Apopka, FL

I've had the honor of being a close friend of Mattheus for many years now. In this book he dives into the process and the power of receiving personal promises and breakthrough. This book will help simplify your faith, warn you of pitfalls and also make you more bold in pursuing God's call for your own life.

– Ben Fitzgerald
Senior Leader, Awakening Europe

This is an important book. I've taught for years that prophetic words are an announcement of God's calling on our lives, and of the beginning of God's processes to prepare us for that calling. I have known Mattheus for many years and have great respect for how he has allowed God to shape his character by submitting to His processes. He truly walks out the message that he brings in *The Process*.

– Dr Arleen Westerhof
Co-lead pastor, God's Embassy, Amsterdam
Co-director, European Prophetic Council

Mattheus van der Steen is my "twin brother", one of my best friends and a fantastic co-worker in the harvest field of the Lord. His faithfulness to God's calling, his humility and his passionate resilience have deeply impacted me. In *The Process*, Mattheus shares much-needed biblical insights and powerful tools on how to hold onto God's promises over your life. I truly believe this book will equip you to become a history-maker.

– Jean-Luc Trachsel
President of the International Association of Healing Ministries

I have known Mattheus for many years as a man of integrity, love and dedication. His new book, *The Process*, will be a great blessing for many people, especially leaders who long to go forward and who really desire to follow Jesus in an even closer way. In good and bad days, Mattheus is faithful to his Lord and Savior and a blessing to many thousands.

– Peter Wenz
Senior pastor, Gospel Forum, Stuttgart

In his latest book, *The Process*, my friend Mattheus van der Steen ingeniously draws parallels between the timeless promises of Scripture and our modern-day journey to fulfillment. His exploration of the biblical notion of promise and its manifestation is a revelation and helps readers to understand that faith is not just about receiving, but also about nurturing and walking a path filled with hope, resilience and transformation. *The Process* is not just a book, it's a spiritual roadmap to the fulfillment of divine promises.

– Caleb Wehrli
Author, speaker, Inspire International and Empowered21

THE PROCESS

MATTHEUS
VAN DER STEEN

ARROWS &
STONES

The Process
— The Journey Between God's Promises Received and Fulfilled

Copyright © 2023 Mattheus van der Steen

Published by Arrows & Stones

Author: Mattheus van der Steen
Editor: Hope Visser
Cover design: Glenn van der Mull
Interior design: Ronald Gabrielsen, 3ig.org

ISBN 978-1-960678-72-0

For Laura

OTHER TITLES
BY THE SAME AUTHOR

Dare to Dream (bestseller)
Dare to Live
Never Ever Give Up
Blood Covenant (forthcoming)

Contents

Foreword

As believers, we have the responsibility and privilege to steward the promises that God has given to us. We do so by treasuring and pondering whatever He has spoken into our lives. The challenge comes when we don't see an immediate fulfillment of what He has promised. It helps to remember that delayed fulfillment is simply gaining interest so that when it is time, it comes fully developed and mature.

The Word of God comes as a seed which is then planted in the soil of our hearts. A heart that is tender receives the word deeply. Transformation happens in a person's life when they give their full and abandoned "yes" to whatever He says. As we hear and believe what God says, we invite His divine empowerment into our lives to bring about the fruitfulness that He intended. And while there is personal delight in fulfilled promises, what matters is that God is glorified through the way we live our lives.

The word of God over your life will always be tested. In Matthew 13, Jesus uses the phrase, "when persecution arises *because of* the word..." (NKJV). This tells me that the Word of God over our lives will attract opposition. In those moments of opposition, we must feed our hearts on what God has said, not on what He hasn't said. On what He is doing, not on what He hasn't done. Like Mary, the mother of Jesus, we must treasure what He has spoken. Feeding our hearts on what God is doing fuels an atmosphere of anticipation in our lives and keeps us constantly reminded of His goodness.

It's critical that as we wait for the fulfillment of what He has spoken, we hold the understanding of God's goodness close to our hearts. I can't afford to let my circumstances or challenges dislodge what I know to be true about God. He is perfectly faithful. Even in mystery or pain, I will not allow myself to entertain ideas about God that question His goodness.

The Process has been written by a man who has lived out the words on these pages. I've had the privilege of watching Mattheus navigate many challenging situations through the years. Each time he walked through them with integrity and faith, not wavering from his devotion to Jesus. I am excited about the impartation of hope that this book carries. If you find yourself growing weary in the process, or if you need to be reminded of the power of God's promises, let this book be a strength and encouragement to you.

Great faith is not the result of striving, but of surrender. Our job in this lifelong journey is to yield our hearts to His words, trusting in His nature as a loving Father. May we be a people who allow the promise of God to shape us, as we joyfully anticipate the fulfillment of what God has declared over each of our lives.

– *Bill Johnson*
Bethel Church, Redding, CA
Author of 'Born for Significance' and 'Strengthen Yourself in the Lord'

Welcome to the process!

You have received a promise from God and you know you are at the point of a breakthrough and then suddenly something goes wrong, the opposite seems to be happening. There are bumps in the road, doors are closing and now it seems very challenging or nearly impossible for that promise to ever be fulfilled.

Have you ever ended up in a situation in which you had to deal with something that you did not start yourself, but it was as if it just fell on top of you? And now you find yourself responsible for a situation that you did not ask for, but you have to act to take care of it?

> ## There is a reason and a purpose behind the pain

Suddenly you find yourself in a crisis, a situation which has the potential to destroy and delay things in your life.

What do you do when you are doing God's will and it seems like God is not helping you?

What do you do when you are doing God's will and the doors are slammed in your face?

What do you do when God promised you something but the opposite is happening?

Welcome to the process! People like to receive a prophetic word but most of the time don't like the process to its fulfillment. I have seen so many people around me go through crises and storms. They have inexplicable things happen to them, and it becomes so disappointing for them that they blame God, others, the situation, or all these things. And I have seen people call things demonic, when in reality it was God allowing things to happen, to bring them to a higher level, to bring them to their calling.

I have been through a number of crises, and overcame several storms, and I felt strongly led by God to write what I have experienced and learned so that I might encourage others to recognize the kind of storm or crises they are going through, and to understand the process and the reason and purpose behind pain, so that you don't give up, so you know you are not alone, and so that you will be able to walk in the calling and in the fullness of all the promises that God has placed on your life.

Join me as I share about going through storms, processes and persevering. Your breakthrough is right around the corner. Giving up now is not an option; you are almost there. Welcome to the process!

It all starts with a promise

When we receive a promise from God, we all go through a process until that promise is fulfilled. There are various phases during that process, and sometimes those phases seem to repeat themselves. But it really all does start with a promise. We all have a promise on our life, whether we are aware of it or not. That promise may come to us in many forms, whether through prophesy, scripture or the manifestation of God's Word in our life. This promise means that God has given you territory to possess. However, unless you understand your inheritance, your territory, your ministry, your calling, you will not see the fullness of God working through you. There is a territory that God has placed in your hands for you to possess by the power of the Holy Spirit.

What is your territory?

Discovering this promise, your territory, your place in life is exciting, exhilarating even! When you know what you are called to do, when you finally realize what you are made for, it brings a level of joy that only God can give. He had plans for you before you were born; you were chosen before creation took place. The God who cared enough to plan you, and everything about you, also had a promise in mind for your life. And the discovery and fulfillment of that promise will make you shine brightly.

The Bible says that we have the light of life on the inside of us (John 8:12). Our light is to shine in the darkness. I have traveled all over the world, and in every city I go to there have been people who come up to me and say: "Mat, it is so dark in this city, it is so good you are here! We have been praying for a move of God." I often answer them that I partner with them in their prayers. "But it is really so dark in this city, there is so much witchcraft, it is a real stronghold!" I have heard this more than a hundred times. I cannot ignore what they are saying by just brushing it aside. But I have seen that the darker the city is, the greater the outpouring is also, the greater the miraculous and the greater the power of God. So if there is a calling, a promise on your life for a particular area, territory, then rest assured that He has not only called you, but given you the tools to do the job.

Because when God decrees something, it is already done. Just as Jesus, the Lamb of God, was slain before the foundations of the earth were laid: "... the Lamb who was slain from the creation of the world" (Rev. 13:8). This is hard to understand with our human minds; how can the Lamb of God be slain before God said: "Let there be light"? We can only understand this through the Spirit who enlightens our minds. When God said, "Let there be light", He had already decreed from eternity into time unending that the Lamb would be slain, that His Son would shed his blood, that He would rise from the dead. This is important, because it shows that when God promises something, when He decrees something, it will happen. He chose you from the foundation of the world. "For he chose us in him before the creation of the world to be holy and blameless in his sight" (Eph. 1:4).

When the right time came for the fulfillment of God's promise, the realization of his decree, His Son in human form here on earth, it happened. Not too soon, not too late, but Jesus came at exactly the right time as a fulfillment of God's promise to all of humankind. "But when the set time had fully come, God sent his Son (...)" (Gal. 4:4a). He arrived at the set time, making God's Word manifest here on earth. When God spoke your name, He spoke from eternity into time, and God sent forth your life, your ministry, your purpose, your destiny. He wants you and me, all of us, to birth our assignment, our calling, what He has already spoken in ages past. That means when the fullness of time has come, which means there are moments and seasons, we must birth what God has already decreed.

If there is something that I have learned in my own life, it's that when it feels like all hell has broken loose, when I feel terribly discouraged, when I don't want to preach another sermon, that is the moment I am about to birth something. It is the moment that God is about to do the greatest miracle in my life. When I am feeling down, God says to me, this is your *kairos* time, your God given moment.

When all hell has broken loose, that is the moment you are about to birth something

The Bible tells us to "not give the devil a foothold" in our lives, to not give him a place (Eph. 4:27). When God gives you a territory to possess, and you have that promise, that prophecy to show you the direction you need to go, it will not go smoothly. The enemy does not want you to move forward and take what is rightfully yours. That is the reason why there is war over your family, war over your ministry, over your church, because the devil does not want to lose ground. God has called you to be a territory taker – "'Not by might nor by power, but by my Spirit,' says the LORD" (Zech. 4:6). All throughout the Bible, God has called people to take their territory, to possess the land. The battle is not about you, or me. The battle is about the territory that you are called to take, and the devil wants it, he is fighting you for your territory.

The Word of God is in you. The promises are in you. The prophecy is in you. The vision is in you. Every promise you have received from God is in you. It is time to take your territory!

Finding your promise

But what if you don't know what your promise is? What if you think you know, but you are not sure? Maybe you received a promise at a conference, a prophetic meeting, a church, but didn't recognize it as such. It is important that we receive teaching not just on the promises of God, and how to recognize them, but it is at least of equal importance to learn how to apply these promises to your life. The promises of God do not just come through other people, through prophetic words or callings. Most of God's promises can be found in the Bible, there are more than 7,000 promises in the Word of God. The Word of God is alive and still active (Heb. 4:12);

The battle is not about you. It is about the territory you are called to take

---

Jesus Himself is the embodiment of the Word. And He said, "Anyone who has seen me, has seen the Father" (John 14:9b) and "no matter how many promises God has made, they are 'Yes' in Christ. And so through him the 'Amen' is spoken by us to the glory of God" (2 Cor. 1:20). What does this mean? It means that we are allowed to apply every promise in the Bible, more than 7,000 promises from God, to ourselves. And we can release those promises through the Spirit of faith. So I pray that every promise over your life, either through prophecy (which must align with the Word of God) or God's Word, be awakened right now in Jesus' Name.

Jesus said we would do greater things than He did (John 14:12).

That is quite something, and to be honest, you do not need a more specific calling to do this! We need to learn how to take the promises that are in God's Word, and stand on them for our own lives. First of all, we must believe the promises. We must then speak the promises out loud and finally, act on them. These are the three key elements when it comes to the promises of God. You do not need to go somewhere for this, you can do it at home. Everyone who has a Bible at home can do this! When you discover these promises of God in His Word, you need to put them into practice. So when you are walking with God, at some point you will receive affirmation of that which was already in your heart.

I remember when I received my first prophetic word. I was in South Africa. I was always in the Word of God, always reading it. And I knew that I was called to the nations. I was called for young people, for revival – I just felt that, sensed that on the inside. When I was baptized in the Holy Spirit this was reaffirmed in my heart, but I had never heard anything about people receiving a prophetic word. I was not raised in a church that taught on these things. I was raised in a Baptist church, and prophetic words were not known at the time. When I was working as a maritime officer on Mercy Ships—I was really young, nineteen years old—a prophet came to visit. I had never heard of such a thing. The prophet was Peter Helms and he started to prophesy over me, about how God would use me all over the world for revival. The awesome thing was that this was a confirmation of that which I already knew in my heart. So I do believe that there can be a real need to receive confirmation of that which is already taking place in your life.

Everyone is called, I am convinced of that. We have all been called, we have all been given the Word of God for our lives. Perhaps you do not know what that is. Maybe no one has ever prophesied over you or your life. That does not matter, just go back to God's Word; that is where your word, your promise is. Everything is contained in his Word. "Go into all the world and preach the gospel to all creation" and go and "look after orphans and widows in their distress" (Mark 16:15; James 1:27). "The LORD will send a blessing on your barns and on everything you put your hand to. The LORD your God will bless you in the land he is giving you" (Deut. 28:8). There are so many ways to find the calling of God for your life, but the most important thing is to have a relationship with God, to read the Word of God as if it was written for you personally. The promises in the Bible come from our God, who is a very personal God. Throughout the Bible we find numerous stories of God getting involved in people's personal lives, and those are the stories about people receiving promises from God.

There is an incredible example in the Bible of what this can look like. The events that took place before the birth of Jesus and the responses of His parents, Joseph and Mary, show what can happen when a promise of God is believed, spoken about and acted upon. They responded to an amazing word of God, a prophecy, and how they responded when faced with opposition, pressure and rejection is extraordinary. Mary was an ordinary young woman when an angel appeared to her and said: "Greetings, you who are highly favored! The Lord is with you. (...) Do not be afraid, Mary; you have found favor with God. You will conceive and give birth to a son, and you are to call him Jesus" (Luke 1:28-31). When Mary heard this, she responded by saying that she was a virgin and unmarried. She was puzzled and wanted to know *how* this would happen!

Perhaps you too have dreams, visions or words from the Lord in your heart and you wonder how any of that will happen. I love how Mary responded. She had real questions but she did not run from the word; she asked a very honest question. I have asked the Lord that same question several times after receiving a prophetic word: "How, Lord?" Not when, or why, but *how?!* When the angel answered her, it was mind-blowing!

He didn't present her with a five-step plan or a ten-year strategy. He said, "Mary, it will happen through the Holy Spirit. The Holy Spirit will come over you and overshadow you. You will conceive without the help of a man and give birth to a son and his name will be Jesus. He will save all of humankind."

Being highly favored and led by the Holy Spirit are two key elements that will lead you into your promised destiny and through the process! You are highly favored and have the option of walking with the Holy Spirit every single day.

Trust the process, trust God

Mary received very good news! The Jewish people had been walking in darkness for 400 years. There was no sound of hope, no words of God for 400 years, and the people were lost in the darkness. They lived in fear and their nation was occupied by the Romans. Suddenly their land had become one big prison. But now, now there was the sound of hope; an angel had a clear message from heaven for a young woman named Mary. Mary did not have a big ministry nor was she well known. Yet she was chosen for this.

However, there is always another side to good news. It seems like a blessing is always accompanied by a burden; as if there is a marriage between blessing and burden. It is possible that people rejoice with you over the blessing or hate you because of the blessing. Many do not recognize that the greater the blessing, the greater the burden. But we know that Jesus already experienced this. Before He rose from the dead and fulfilled His mission, He too went through very difficult processes, just like most men and women of God, who often go through processes from a young age. In the end it is about learning how to grab hold of the promises, and then hang onto them when everything around us seems to scream that none of these promises will ever happen.

In the following chapters we will take a look at several biblical examples, as well as examples from my own life, so that we can discover together how we can get from the promise to the fulfillment of that promise. Yes, there is a process in-between, and when the promise is fulfilled, there will be other challenges, but right now, if you are going through a storm, then I want to encourage you. When you are in a deep, dark well, and the promise you have received from God only seems like a vague and distant memory, then I want you to try this. I have written down a few simplified truths for you to use. I want to encourage you to read through these every day, and maybe even more frequently, to remind yourself of the truth.

The truth is that you are valuable in God's eyes. He really has given you promises and He is still at work, though you may not see it.

> » It is not important to know all the facts, but it is important to choose to keep moving forward in faith.
> » I am loved by God. There may be days that are a struggle, days when I feel weak. But there is never a day when God is not there. His love keeps me going.
> » Never stop praying, never stop believing, never give up.
> » Stress makes us believe that everything has to happen now. Faith reassures us that everything happens in God's time.
> » Diamonds form under pressure, olives are pressed to get oil, a seed must be broken in order to grow.
> » Trust the process, trust God.
> » The same power that raised Christ from the dead, lives inside of me (Rom. 8:11).
> » Though I do not understand everything, I will choose to trust God.

THE

PRO

CESS

(1)

YOU HAVE A PROMISE

What happens next?

Whether it is a prophetic word, a dream, impression or a word in the Bible, you have found or received certain promises and you just know that God has given them to you. So now what?

The first thing the enemy will try to do is to rob the seed of that promise. I have discovered that the people in your life are not always the ones who will encourage you and cheer you on in pursuing the fulfillment of your promise. First of all, they will not have received the same revelation from God and secondly, you will often find that they respond from a place of pain and jealousy. So when I have received a promise, I don't broadcast it to the whole world. Instead, because it is so fragile, so precious, I only share it with my wife. We will pray about it together and we will proclaim it.

Trials and tests are a joyous thing when you understand the reason behind them

---

This is very important as "the power of life and death" are in the tongue (Prov. 18:21). It is in the words we speak. By saying the promise out loud, we speak life into the promise we have received. And when the enemy comes to sow seeds of unrest and to bring doubt and unbelief by whispering, "See, you can't do this", or "You misunderstood God's words", I always go back to the promise. That is why it is of vital importance to write down your promises. Don't just allow it to float around in your head, but write it down. Write the vision and "make it plain" and stand on the promises you have been given (Hab. 2:2).

There is something else that I want to mention. When you have received a prophetic word, you need to ask yourself if that word is a NOW word. Is it something that is going to take place now? How many of us, when we have received a prophetic word, have ended up in a situation that seems to be the opposite of that which was prophesied? What is the first thing that comes to mind? Were they wrong? Are they a false prophet? Perhaps the word was not correct?

I have often seen people, especially young people, who have received a wonderful word or a beautiful prophecy in a safe and blessed environment in conferences, churches or Bible schools. They are in this amazing bubble of anointed atmosphere, and when they leave that atmosphere, they end up in situations they were not prepared for.

We need to prepare a generation through training, speaking and writing, teaching them how to deal with pressure, rejection, how to endure difficult processes and tests, so that they will not be surprised when these things occur. They should actually be surprised when these things *don't* happen! They will experience it as pure joy! Imagine seeing your trials and tests as a joyous thing because you understand the reason behind why you are going through such things. James was very straightforward about this:

> Consider it pure joy, my brothers and sisters, whenever you face trials of many kinds, because you know that the testing of your faith produces perseverance. Let perseverance finish its work so that you may be mature and complete, not lacking anything.
> – JAMES 1:2-4

Timing is everything

I think that timing is crucial. What I have often seen is that when a promise is received, there is a period of time in which the opposite seems to occur. That is the waiting room, where nothing seems to be happening, but God is actually at work behind the scenes. I have often experienced this myself, that things got so quiet that I started to wonder if God was doing anything at all in my situation. But He was always at work for me. That is fascinating.

Being patient is very important too, and trusting that God will fulfill his promise to you. Our part in all this, our responsibility, is to remain standing on that promise, whether it seems like something is happening or not. Lack of faith and fear are the two components that turn the fruitful ground of God's Kingdom to barren ground, preventing any growth from happening. Abraham's story and the promises he received from God have always been very encouraging to me. Abraham knew that his God was a God of covenant. The covenant that was made between God and him, and the consequences of that covenant, are pretty amazing (Heb. 6:13).

We live in a culture of contracts; our society really does not understand the whole concept of covenant anymore. Abraham knew this: "God, you have given me a promise. I will be a father of a nation. But I am infertile and old, how is this supposed to happen?" Then God said: "I am going to make a covenant with you, a blood covenant." Because of the culture and the era that he lived in, Abraham understood what a blood covenant meant: Both parties were bound to this covenant; there was no way to get out of it. Abraham realized: "If I do not keep to this covenant, keep these promises, then all of these curses will come upon me. But if I do keep to this covenant, then all of these blessings will come upon me." God, who was the other party in this covenant, had to keep to His promises as well, because it goes against His nature not to keep His promises. So Abraham knew that God would uphold his part of the covenant.

We can read in the New Testament how Abraham held onto the promises of God without doubting and without entertaining the spirit of unbelief. It is powerful! And I think there is something in our current culture, this thought that: "If God does not answer within a certain amount of time, I will give up and start looking for something new." That shows a total lack of character. To continue trusting God, thanking Him for his character, remain standing on His promises—that is a character trait that our generation needs to train themselves in. The story of Abraham goes on to tell that God did in fact fulfill His promise to Abraham, but it took a very long time.

Don't give up

When the Lord gives you a word, He knows what you are going through at the time, or what you will be dealing with in the future. And He is loving enough to give you a word of life before the people around you or the situations you are in start to give you words of discouragement, death and destruction. So when the opposite happens in your life after you have a received a prophetic word, write the word down, share it only with those who are for you, and proclaim it out loud every day of your life: "Lord, You said ... !"

Just like Timothy was encouraged by Paul:

> Timothy, my son, I am giving you this command in keeping with the prophecies once made about you, so that by recalling them you may fight the battle well, holding on to faith and a good conscience ...
> – 1 TIMOTHY 1:18-19a

Don't give up. Fight the good fight.

When the time comes

I do believe there is also a fullness of time. What I mean by that is there is a season in which all of the promises of God are fulfilled. That is the fullness of time. You can see this in the story of Joseph in Egypt, in the story of Abraham, in the story of Mary, and in the life of Peter. There was a certain season in which all of the promises that were on their lives all seemed to be fulfilled at the same time. Actually, that is the same as the story of Jesus. The first thirty years of his life were not

very visible. Then for three years He was in the spotlight. That
is because of the fullness of time. So if you are reading this
book, and you are not yet living in the fullness of time, then
know this: God is at work for you. The best thing you can do
is remain in His presence. Thank Him for the promise.

Thankfulness is one of the most important weapons that
God has given you. Jehoshaphat chose to praise God for the
victory over his enemies before it ever even occurred. That is
the amazing thing about Christians, that we have the opportunity to be thankful in all circumstances (1 Thess. 5:18),
to thank God for His fulfillment of promises, before we
have seen any fulfillment of promise in our life. When we do
this, it draws heaven to us. Thanking Him ahead of time, for
something that has yet to take place—that is faith (Rom. 4:17).
I am convinced that faith brings about our hope, the things
we hope for, and makes them a reality. There are many things
that people do not know about, things that have already been
prepared in the invisible realm. "Now faith is confidence in
what we hope for and assurance about what we do not see"
(Heb. 11:1). Through faith you bring things from the unseen
realm into reality. Faith is so very important, so do not allow
yourself to get discouraged.

Believing, speaking and acting

I believe that you, as you walk in your calling, will at some
point receive a confirmation of that which is already alive
in your heart. I want to share an example with you of how
this can be put into practice. At the moment I am writing
this book, we are living in a time of war in Europe, Ukraine
has been invaded by a neighboring nation, many places have
been bombed, there is a lot of misery, need and brokenness.
And I have been called to go to the nations to bring hope and
the power of the Holy Spirit, to bring Jesus to those very places
where there is war, where nations are closed to the gospel.

These places are not easy to go to or to work in. That's where it starts, actually. Most people are afraid to go to a warzone. A seed of faith to go to Ukraine was placed in my heart. But due to the current situation, it was very hard to go there. You could not just take a flight. But that seed was in my heart.

There is a season in which all the promises of God are fulfilled

Now, I had a choice: I could allow that seed to fall into my soul. "Wait a minute. First of all, my wife is pregnant; secondly, I have a big conference coming up that I have a lot to prepare for; thirdly, there are a lot of upcoming changes in our life. I don't have the money to pay for this!" And last but not least: "It is really dangerous." Lack of faith, unbelief, worries. This is all human reasoning. "How am I ever going to do this?"

Or, I could allow that seed to take root in my spirit. I have learned that if I have a seed of faith, I need to bring it to God first. "Lord, would You protect that seed? I want to act on this. So I will believe it, say it out loud and act on it." Acting on a promise, on a word that has been given, is very important. Many people get stuck in the phase of believing and then speaking out the promise, but then the seed of doubt from the enemy wiggles its way into their life: "I can't do this; this isn't going to work." As a result, they never act on the word. One of the biggest keys I can offer those reading this book is: Start to act on the promise that God has given you.

So what does that look like? What does it look like to act on a seed of promise? In my case, it looked like this: I picked up my phone and sent a message to a pastor I knew in Ukraine. "I feel like I need to be available to you. Can I come?" He responded: "That is fantastic, Mattheus. But you do know it is really dangerous here? Are you sure?" To make a long story short, we got things moving. We decided that I would go to Kiev. I did not have the money, but I did write a newsletter.

Because God had spoken, I was sure I was doing the right thing. We went there in faith, God supplied a car, God made many different churches available and in six days we were able to minister to 9,000-10,000 people. That became a historical journey as a result. And we saw the mighty power of God manifest there. Why am I telling you this? I could have stayed home. I could have said, "I believe this word, this seed, but God needs to do it." But I don't think it works like that. God has spoken, and we have the responsibility to believe it, speak it out in faith, and then act on it. So I went.

People asked me: "Wow, weren't you afraid?" And before I left, they asked me, "Are you sure about this?" I knew, however, that God had spoken to me. The most amazing thing was that I had told the Lord, and the next day I went to Laura, my wife, and I said, "This is the seed that the Lord spoke to me, would you pray about it as well?" I always involve my wife in the process. She is my "second Holy Spirit", she is my radar. She decided to pray about it and she said, "I would rather you don't go. I am pregnant. If something happens to you then I will be left with four children and a house to pay for. What would I do?" But then she said, "I am a woman of God, I won't speak from my soul. I want to pray about it and receive confirmation from God." The next morning she woke up, and opened her phone to where there is a daily Bible verse. And that morning, instead of the Bible verse, it said: "Visit Ukraine." It was probably some kind of strange commercial; we are still not sure what it was. But to Laura the message was clear: "He has to go to Ukraine." We made a screenshot, it was a clear answer.

You believe it, you speak it out together, and you act on it. Those three things.

Community is vital

Many people hear the promise, through a prophetic word, for example, but are not aware of the process that happens for that prophetic word to be fulfilled. You need to learn about the purpose of the process. Why are you going through this storm? If you know why, then you may find that you are blessed by the process.

I do believe we are not called to run the race alone. We need people around us who encourage us, pray for us, and are honest with us. But what if you do not have people like that? Sometimes I meet people who say, "I do not have anyone praying for me." I tell them, "That is not true. Jesus is your intercessor (Rom. 8:34; Heb. 7:25). He is praying for you right now." That is a huge comfort. He intercedes for you. Jesus never sent His disciples out into the world alone. So I think it is important that you find a community. A community of people of faith and promises. I do not want to distinguish between Christians, I really dislike that. But I can spot them in a crowd. If I am in a community where faith is preached, where promises are preached, or if I am in a community where people speak from their soul, from a place of neediness, a place of suffering, I can tell the difference.

So find yourself a community that is healthy, read books on faith, pray that God will give you someone, a friend, like Jonathan was for David, a healthy relationship. Someone who encourages you, strengthens you, reminds you of the promises of God for your life. And the fact is that sometimes you are in a season in which everything seems to be broken. I too have been through a season like that, in which everything you have built up over the years seems to come crashing down in a moment like a house of cards and you feel like you have to start all over again. That is a soul perspective. God sees it in a very different way.

Never giving up

I have written a book with the title *Never ever give up*. Just keep on walking. You don't need to run, don't need to prove yourself, just keep moving forward. Keep standing on the promises of God, even though you are discouraged, though you feel like you cannot go on anymore. Moses too was discouraged; he couldn't go on. But praise God, Aaron and Hur were there to raise his arms (Ex. 17:12). At this time I pray for you, dear reader, that someone would come alongside you to support you. I do believe that God will give you that. He also says: "I will not allow you to be tempted beyond what you can bear" (1 Cor. 10:13).

> ### Start to act on the promise
> ### that God has given you

There have been times that I cried out, "I cannot bear this!" There have been three times in my life in which I thought that I could not bear the load. And I couldn't, but He was there with His peace, with His strong shoulders. I cannot look back on those times without seeing God there too, next to me. I felt it intensely, the heavens seemed to be made of copper, but I refused to doubt God's promises. I refused to stop praying, stop reading the Bible, stop worshiping. Those things are really very important. But I can imagine that people have been in that situation for a long time, and they have become very discouraged. They no longer have hope. And though it may sound harsh, no matter how you feel, you are responsible for how you deal with those emotions. Please find the right people, and the right place so that you can be helped, when you no longer have the strength to go on.

Every morning when I awaken, I always ask the Holy Spirit to enter my room and I imagine Jesus standing in front of me. And then I read the Word of God in His presence. I have plenty of challenges in my life and if there is one thing I have learned it is this: Instead of running around and telling everyone about it in panic mode, I first write things in my prayer journal. I list the need or challenges. God has called me, but I do not have an answer for this. So I go to God's Word to find a promise from God that relates specifically to the problem or challenge that I am facing at that moment. That is why it is so important that we know God's Word really well. Because the better we know His Word, the less effort it costs us to remember God's promises. I believe it, I speak it out and I act on it.

Here is a very simple example of this. I get up in the morning, and I need to go somewhere to speak, but my left shoulder is hurting terribly. The first thing I will do is to go downstairs to my prayer journal, which I use a lot, and write what the promise of God is in this situation. "By his wounds we are healed." That is a promise, from Isaiah 53:5. I believe the Word and I apply it to my life. I place my hands on myself and I speak it out in the Name of Jesus: "This pain has no right to my body." I believe it and I act on it, as if the promise has already been fulfilled. So I thank the Lord for the miracle. I move my shoulder, and I have often noticed that the pain is gone immediately. But sometimes the pain remains until I am actually on stage, and then I notice that it is gone. This may seem like something small, but I do believe we need to focus more on the promises of God in His Word, and apply them to our own lives. This is something we can all do. This is something you can do at home. Jesus has called on all of us to lay hands on the sick (Mark 16:18).

David did not talk about how big and impressive Goliath, the problem, was. David proclaimed how big God was and defeated Goliath. Read 1 Samuel 17!

Without our focus on God and His promises, we will never get through the process. Some words are for now, and some are for later in life. But whether it is for now or later, there is usually a process connected to that word, before we will see the fulfillment of that prophetic word or promise in our life.

THE PROCESS

What does that look like?

I want to invite you to join me on this amazing, yet vulnerable and sometimes painful, journey through the process. Let us go on this adventure together and as you read this book, you will understand the process through the context of the stories. All of this is with the end goal in mind that we will become more like Him, more like His image, and to gain understanding that there is a reason behind the pain and the storms that we sometimes go through. It is a fact that there is a word from God, a destiny and calling on your life. This calling and destiny will always be tested. And that testing will lead us to and through a personal process. Sadly, I have seen many people give up during their personal process before seeing the fulfillment of the promise.

We all want a word from God, but there is a process between receiving that word from God and the fulfillment of it. If you cannot understand the process or why you are going through it, you will give up. The process starts the moment you experience your first disappointment. "I received this promise, and now what? I was expecting something different!"

If you know you are called by God, but it seems as though the opposite is taking place, when you experience abnormal pressure, rejection, betrayal, when you're wounded and at your breaking point, then this book is for you. You are reading this at just the right time. When you feel like you will break, or have been broken, when you are under pressure, or oppression, or alone in the darkness, then you are in a powerful place for transformation. I cannot take away your pain, or stop the things that are happening to you. But it will make the process lighter and easier if you know the reason behind part of the process.

Transition, another name for process

We could also describe process as a transition. There are different kinds of transitions. For instance, there can be a sudden transition due to the death or sickness of a partner or family member, a new job, moving to a new home, a new assignment, or the transition of walking into the fullness of your calling.

Some transitions are caused by you, others are caused by people around you, by circumstances, by God, or even by the devil who is trying to attack you and lead you to a transition in the wrong direction. In all of these transitions certain things happen, and I want to take the time to explain to you what is happening when you go through a transition.

Remember that our ultimate transition on earth is the one described in Genesis 1:26 when God said: "Let us make mankind in our image, in our likeness ..." All of us are in the continuing process and transition of being transformed into the image and likeness of God. Everything in our character, lifestyles and our issues that do not fit this image and likeness of God needs to be transformed so that we become more like Him. Many people describe the season they are going through as a process of transition. Being in transition most of the time causes stress and pressure. It is a time of pruning and learning to trust. Learning to walk in faith and not leaning on your own understanding is part of the transition (Prov. 3:5). Transition can be wonderful and ugly at the same time, a blessing and burden rolled into one.

The in-between-time

To let go of the old and move into the new is the most difficult part. It is a time when what worked in the old season will not work in the new season. Sometimes you will be forced to leave the old season behind. It is the season that is familiar to you, where you know how to survive, how to celebrate. In a way, the old season represents all that we know. We know how to live our lives and how to navigate that old season. When we have to leave that behind there is a feeling of excitement, as well as mourning, a letting go of the past. And then we are in the in-between-time, no longer in the old season, the comfortable place, and not yet arrived in the new season.

> Transition is a process in which
> our soul becomes more like the finished
> work of Jesus

You don't know yet what that new period, the new season will look like. When you are in the transition, you cannot see what will or will not be in that new season. You can only guess how far along you are in the transition, as there are no anchor points; nothing is fixed in place and you don't know how much further you need to go. It is at this point, with all of the unknowns ahead of you, that your character and your faith will help you to keep going—straight through this difficult and yet very important in-between-time. I believe that the hardest and most uncomfortable part about this time is when the foundation is being laid for the next step, the next season; just as in the story of Joseph and Mary, which we will look at in more depth later on in this book—they had received a prophetic word, Mary conceived through the Holy Spirit, and they left all of the old behind. But before the word could be fulfilled, there was an in-between-time, when they began to walk in the direction of the unknown, not knowing that God would provide everything they would need when they entered the start of their new season: A place to stay, shepherds, wise men and provision for the period ahead.

Nature's example

There is a beautiful example of the transition period, the process, in nature. This is when a caterpillar is transformed into a butterfly. There are lessons that we can learn from this process. And what we learn we can use as tools to navigate our own season of transformation.

First you have the transition phase. This is the most interesting stage of butterfly development, which seems catastrophic from the caterpillar's perspective. A caterpillar going through this phase will completely lose itself and everything it has ever known. This is not unlike what we go through during our own transition.

When the tiny caterpillar reaches maturity and can no longer eat, it simply dangles from a branch and twists a protective cocoon around itself so that it can rest safely and digest all the food consumed in the previous stage. This phase can last several weeks, a month or even longer. Some caterpillar species have a pupal stage that lasts two years. And in the same way this phase takes time, our transitions take time. They are not over in a day, a week, or sometimes even a year.

First, the caterpillar digests itself, releasing enzymes to dissolve all its tissues. If you cut open a cocoon at the right time, a caterpillar soup substance comes out. There is nothing formed, no context or shape.

This is exactly how most people describe the season of transition. It looks and feels like soup. No structure, nothing tangible to hold on to, emotions all over the place and feelings of insecurity, excitement and anxiety. There are questions and sleepless nights, stress and lack of rest. There can also be moments of peace, but mostly it is turmoil. One moment you feel like you are close to God, the next moment it is so hard to hear His voice or understand Him. You feel like you are on a rollercoaster. It feels like you have one foot in the old and the other stepping into the new, yet you are not moving forward. It is like trying to climb a mountain as you travel up from the valley. One leg is downhill and the other leg is uphill. Until you take the next step, you are not moving forward.

Rebuilding and restructuring

After the cocoon of the caterpillar has been formed, its body will release special enzymes, that will dissolve cells in the caterpillar's muscles and organs. Everything will dissolve and change, except for the most vital life-supporting cells. Then, a group of specialized cells get to work, rebuilding and restructuring the insect's new body and wings in just a short period of time. These cells are also called the imaginal disks. Those disks use the protein-rich soup around them to form a butterfly from the formless fluid.

This phase is the one we misunderstand the most when we are in it. We usually take the caterpillar perspective and view this stage as a crisis or downturn, trying to advance our growth at any cost. This process of letting go of something to hold on to something else means that for a period we can feel that we are not holding on to anything. Everything the caterpillar was and everything the butterfly will be is in the cocoon, but one shape has to give itself up for another to appear.

Do not give up during the transition phase. This is one of the most important aspects of the butterfly principle. There must be time for rest and withdrawal during the growth process. This is the season where its important you rest and that you allow the Lord to fight your battles. Because in most cases, in this season you are emotionally drained and tired and even battling with low self-esteem or feeling like you are disqualified.

However, this is all part of the process. You must let go of the old in order to grab hold of the new. But if you were to see that in a slow-motion film, you would see that there is actually a moment in which you are holding on to nothing. Just like the caterpillar transforming into a butterfly, there is a phase in which it is no longer a caterpillar, and not yet a butterfly. The in-between-time.

> ### Without our focus on God and His promises, we will never get through the process

We will need to trust God in this time. He is the architect. He has a plan for us in the middle of the mess; if we only let Him in and continue to trust Him, He will bring about what He has planned for us. That will be a journey of discovery for us as well. We will discover who we are, how we were created by God, and what His plan is for us. But that cannot happen without a process, without a transition. Without letting go. We seem to think that we can just go from one mountaintop to the next, but forget that there is a valley in-between. The process is needed in order to bring us from the promise—which may seem quite abstract when we first receive it—to the fulfillment of that promise in our life.

The Bible school bubble

Bible school students typically find themselves in a bubble. It is a time of being in a group of like-minded people, and a relatively safe environment. Perhaps we could see this as the caterpillar phase, happily munching on the leaves of God's Word, growing and learning. Often students will receive promises and prophecies during their time at school. However, we need to do a better job of preparing the students for the process that lies between the receiving of a promise and the fulfillment of that promise.

I highly support and encourage going to a Bible school. What I do often see, though, is that the students are in a certain atmosphere, a protective bubble, as it were. But then when it's graduation day and it's time they go back to society, back to "normal" life, they are no longer in that protective atmosphere. They are totally unprepared for heading back into society, and holding on to those promises and prophecies that were given during their time at Bible school proves to be very difficult. They suddenly find themselves in a "soup", no structure, nothing familiar and no indication of that which is to come. They often fall back into old patterns and habits, as they no longer have something to hold on to (the structure that was provided for them). They are no longer radically devoted to submerging themselves in the Word of God, they are no longer surrounded by like-minded people, their bubble is gone. And many of the promises that the students received at the Bible school have not yet become part of their lives. It takes time, it is a process, and it will come about in their lives, but not right away.

I do believe that students need better preparation for this; that they need to hear that, yes, these are amazing and beautiful dreams and promises that have been given to you, but there will first be a process, a transition, before those dreams and promises are fulfilled in your life. And that process does not have to be unpleasant, but it is certainly not always nice or comfortable.

Transition takes character

Mary had received a promise, and directly after that promise she was plunged into a transition process. Suddenly she found herself pregnant, carrying the Son of God in her womb. There must have been whispers and stares, as she was not yet married to Joseph when God placed Jesus in her womb. Then when she was far along in her pregnancy, she was sitting on the back of a donkey for seven long days. That must have been so uncomfortable for her. Yet she showed her character by not complaining, not defending herself, but instead carrying the Savior of the world in her womb with grace and dignity.

It seems to be a reoccurring pattern in the Bible: Men and women who receive a calling from God and yet they are somehow in a season in which the opposite of that calling and promise seems to be happening. I personally think that a lot of this is to form our character and to teach us to trust God, instead of leaning on that gifted speaker, that amazing atmosphere, that wonderful church, or that generous person who has a whole lot of money. What it all comes down to, when everything else is stripped away, is that your character is formed when it is just you and God. Where you learn to trust Him though your circumstances say otherwise. Though everything else seems to contradict his promise, He is still at work.

Or what about the life of Abraham? The fulfillment of the promise for Abraham took a very long time. Abraham knew the promise, but it took years for it to be fulfilled. He was a hundred years old. The Bible tells us that he did not lose faith. He kept believing, despite what seemed to be a delay in the fulfillment. I think that if you start to appreciate the process and the reason behind it, you will find joy, and be able to remain faithful, like Abraham. You will also allow the Holy Spirit to form your character as you are in the process.

Spiritual muscles

There are seasons, both in the spiritual and the natural—fall, winter, spring and summer. And those are reoccurring cycles. Sometimes we go through processes that are not bad or stressful, but can actually be nice. Just look at our bodies, for example: I go to the gym and I enjoy training. However, if I have not been for a while, I need to do the exact same exercises to trigger my muscles. If I have been gone for two or three weeks, then I notice my muscle mass starts to shrink. But there is also such a thing as muscle memory, which means that after two or three weeks of no training, I need to restart the process. However, once I start to the do the familiar exercises, my body recognizes and knows what is happening. I need to start the process up again by first doing warming-up exercises, increasing the weights, paying attention to my diet, etc. I can't just stay away for a few weeks and then jump straight into heavy-duty training. No, there is a process that you need to slowly ease back into, a pattern.

I believe it works the same way for faith. If you have not read your Bible for a few weeks, have not spent time with God, you will need to slowly ease back into training your spiritual faith muscles. Your spirit needs to be trained, just like your body. Your character needs to be formed, and this too takes time. We do live in a time when many people, especially young people, want to see direct results. And that just isn't possible, and if it were, it would be very bad for us. There are no quick results when you are building muscle mass in the natural, even if you think using special powders and supplements will give you fast results. It is a process. The muscles are already there, they just need to be told what to do. Consistently. Every single day. The same applies to our spiritual faith muscles. God has given us the "muscles", the spiritual gifts, we just need to train them. And that takes time and practice.

I sometimes meet people who have great plans and ideas, but I can sense they have not yet been through a process. Or they received a prophetic word but are not willing to do the work connected to that prophetic word. We often do not want to hear that. That is the reason why some people give up halfway through the process, because they don't want to pay the price of going through that process. You need to be consistent, even when the results are not (yet) visible. You have to value the process, because sore muscles are no fun.

My son Zephaniah weighs more than I do. He exercises a lot at the gym. He often has sore muscles; I can tell when he is at home and I see he is hurting. But he enjoys the process. He will be exhausted, worn out and in pain, yet he loves it because he knows that there is a reason, a goal behind the process. It will make him stronger and increase his muscle mass.

So when we go through life, with aching faith muscles from consistent use, I do not think that is a bad thing. Our muscles need to be trained; our faith needs to be trained. And that can only happen by taking a step and (willingly) going through exercises or circumstances that are not always nice. I don't really like having heavy weights on my legs during exercises, and after lifting ten to twelve times, I am worn out. But if I am consistent, my muscles can gradually bear more weight.

Season of process

So when you enter the season of process, don't doubt the promise, even though it is not (yet) visible. You need to make sure you have an attitude of persistence to build your faith muscles, and act on the promise that has been given to you. David acted like a king before he was one. Everything in his character testified to consistent exercise of his faith muscles. After he had been given the prophecy that he would be king, his father sent him to see his brothers who were on the frontline. Upon arrival he saw Goliath. And while others around him talked about how big Goliath was, David talked about how great his God was. That was the only reason he ran towards Goliath. He was already acting like a man of God, already acting like a king. I think that that is very important, that you already start to act on the promise that you have received from God, without wanting to be "in position" first. Act like you are already king without having to be on the throne first. God will place you on the throne when it is the right time. But until then, act like you are royalty.

If you have been called as an evangelist, then you will naturally want to bring people to Jesus every day. Not just when you are standing on a stage in front of a crowd. So dress (and act) for the job you want, not for the job you have.

Your character is formed when it is just you
and God, when everything else is stripped away

The enemy is not afraid of people, but he is afraid of people discovering who they are in Christ. He is terrified they will discover the authority they have already been given, and start to walk in the calling that God has placed on their lives. Satan will do anything to sow seeds of doubt in order to block the season of transition, or twist it in the wrong direction. One of the first things he will do is bring people and circumstances into your life that will communicate unbelief. There will be lies and words of doubt: "See, your God is not healing you."

When Jesus hung on the cross, people were taunting Him, saying that He could not even save Himself (let alone someone else). Yet that was the very thing He came to do, to save us. But the enemy took His calling, His destiny, and twisted it and tried to at least make everyone else doubt, even if he could not get Jesus to doubt. One of the first things the enemy will do is attempt to plant a seed of doubt or fear. Now, he cannot plant that seed in your spirit, because as a Christian your spirit is connected to the Holy Spirit. But he can plant it in your soul. Your soul is the domain where satan can still exert control over you. Transition is when our soul enters a process in which it becomes more and more like the finished work of Jesus that is in our spirit. Through all these transitions and processes, the influence and control of the evil one on our life and ministry will diminish.

Just like transition is another word for process, some of the seasons in our life can also be seen as storms. I have gone through a number of storms in my own life. Some of these storms were so extreme I thought I would lose everything. A number of beautiful and painful processes also started in these storms. That is why I want to take a look at the different kinds of storms in the coming chapters, and how we can get through them. Because there is no alternative than to get through the storm. We cannot sit still when it gets hard. The caterpillar cannot remain in its cocoon as caterpillar soup forever. It has to rebuild to eventually break out and fly.

3

STORMS

It's all part of the process

I have found that storms often wash over my life after God has spoken a word to me or through a prophecy that was connected to countries and influence. Just like what happened when the storm suddenly appeared on the lake as Jesus sailed to the man who was possessed by a legion of demons. Jesus knew God's promises that were on his life, that He would bring freedom to the captives. But the enemy caused a storm to take place, to try to prevent Jesus from getting to the man who needed His help so desperately. Jesus spoke to the storm and after all the winds and the waves obeyed and calmed down the fulfillment of God's promise came to pass; the man who the world thought was as good as dead, living among the tombs, was finally delivered (Mark 4–5). I started to discover that there is a biblical pattern that takes place after the word of God has been spoken over a person.

> ## The heroes of faith needed the storms in order to reach their destiny

Hebrews 11 lists heroes of the faith in the Old Testament. They are not called heroes because of the large number of great acts of faith, but because they continued to believe in the face of opposition and difficult circumstances. That is called a steadfast faith and that is what enabled them to experience the amazing things of God. In spite of the storms, they continued to trust God and move forward. These heroes had an active faith instead of a passive faith.

I want to take you on a journey to help you understand why some storms take place in our life and to show you that all of these storms, when you have passed through them in

the right way, will lead you to the fulfillment of your promises
and to walking in your calling and destiny. Because there
is a reason for these storms.

Storms are needed

Hebrews 11 proclaims that it was by faith that these heroes
remained standing during their storms. I think there was
even more to it. I think they actually needed those storms
in order to reach their destiny. I do not know if Peter would
have become the rock on which the Church was built if it
had not been for the storm that he went through after Jesus
had proclaimed: "And I tell you that you are Peter, and on this
rock I will build my church, and the gates of Hades will not
overcome it" (Matt. 16:18). I am not convinced that David
would have become king if he had not first defeated the giant
Goliath. And just as Hebrews 11 states: "By faith Abraham,
when God tested him, offered Isaac as a sacrifice. He who
had embraced the promises was about to sacrifice his
one and only son, even though God had said to him, 'It is
through Isaac that your offspring will be reckoned.' Abraham
reasoned that God could even raise the dead, and so in a manner
of speaking he did receive Isaac back from death" (Heb. 11:17-
19). I am not certain that Abraham would have become the
father of a nation if he had not first been willing to sacrifice
his son. And would he have been willing to let Lot choose the
better portion of land, as we read in Genesis 13, if he had not
believed that God would help him through that? The storms
these heroes of the faith went through were needed to increase
their trust and faith in God.

Cows and buffalos

The natural world shows a beautiful example of this too. When
there is a storm on the way on the prairies of the United States,
you can see it coming at a great distance. Cows and buffalos

sense the storm before it arrives, before it is even visible, and they both respond to it, although in a very different manner. Cows feel the storm coming and take off running. They run as fast and as far as they can, trying to stay ahead of the storm. But the storm always catches up to them and overtakes them. The cows keep on running in fear, trying to get away from the storm. They totally exhaust themselves, but keep on running. What they do not realize is that the storm takes even longer for them because they run with the storm, instead of just simply standing still and letting it wash over them.

Buffalos also feel the storm coming, and they too start moving. But in contrast to the cows, buffalos charge towards the storm. And when the storm reaches them, they keep on going, heads lowered, straight into the storm. Eventually they come out on the other side of the storm, far less exhausted and fearful, and "their" storm didn't last half as long as the storm for the cows. It was the same storm, but the duration of the storm for the cows was longer than for the buffalos.

So, if we have to go through a storm, then we can learn from this that it is better to face the storm head-on and charge right on through it, instead of attempting to run from it because we think that the storm is so unfair, or because we feel we did not deserve to go through a storm like that, or whatever reason we may think of to tell ourselves why we should not be in a storm in the first place. It is clear that we need to go through the storm. So let's take a look at how we can get through those storms in the best possible way.

Spirit, soul and body

When we go through a storm or a crisis in our life, it is important to realize that it influences our spirit, soul and body. How we respond to crises, storms and difficulties that leave us bruised and beaten, feeling betrayed and rejected, with wounds and aches, can make all the difference in how we come out on the other side. It is vital to understand how our spirit, soul and body work together and it can literally be life-changing.

Humans are spiritual beings, just like God because God is Spirit. We humans are made up of three interwoven parts, each with its own task and function. Your spirit has a spiritual personality, your soul has a natural personality. It is often hard to distinguish between spirit and soul, and the same applies to where the soul ends and the body starts. God is a triune being; we cannot clearly see where the Son stops and the Father or Spirit start. In the same way, we cannot see where our spirit stops and our soul and body start.

How we respond to crises makes all the difference in how we come out on the other side

Your soul is your human side, it contains your will, your character, your personality, your emotions and feelings, skills, thoughts and your mind. With your soul you are in contact with the visible world and with the people around you. In other words, your soul is formed by the things and events that you experience in life. Your upbringing and the things you experience as a child, teenager and young adult, but also later in life, shape certain habits, patterns and the way you think, speak, act and react. It may be that your soul has been damaged, injured or traumatized by violent and difficult circumstances or events in your life. Your soul can also become disappointed and bitter, and because of that you can react to things happening around you from your soul in a way that does not correspond with your spirit or with you as a mature Christian. All these things take place in our soul, which is our human and natural side.

Most times when we go through a process of transformation, a storm or a crisis, our soul will respond in agony, anxiety, stress and all kinds of emotions. We must train our spirit, which is connected to and filled with the Holy Spirit, to overcome all these soul emotions. If we can see that our soul emotions are separate from our spirit, then we are able to walk through the process a lot more easily and happily. Many people don't realize that they have a spirit which is stronger than their soul emotions. When your soul emotions speak the loudest in crises, it can get very messy and ugly. When that happens, I see people give up or they stop running the race with God because of their soul pain and emotions. And again, this pain in their soul and emotions are real, and can be very agonizing and awful. Realizing that your spirit is stronger and can, to a certain degree, overrule the pain and hurt coming from your soul is not the same as ignoring what is actually happening to your soul.

Know your storm (and enemy)

Before we get into looking at how we can remain standing in faith (or even charging headfirst into an oncoming storm like a buffalo), to keep on going during a crisis, conflict, betrayal, inflicted wounds, brokenness and rejection, I need to explain why it is so important to know who and what is behind this season. In other words: What kind of storm have you ended up in? Who is responsible for this storm? It is very important to understand this, so that you know *why* you are going through such a storm.

We experience storms in every area of our lives—mental, physical, emotional and spiritual. These are the times when, just as the weather can change unexpectedly, things can un-expectedly change in our lives, and our usual patterns and behavior are disrupted by circumstances which are in many cases beyond our control. The storms of life can vary by type and duration. For example, Abraham's wife, Sarah, faced the storm of barrenness over a long period of time, but it came to an end through the spirit of faith. Leah's storm was that her husband, Jacob, did not love her, but she overcame in the end because God gave her favor.

Now, in my experience there are three different types of storms that could occur. There are storms in life that we have created ourselves based on unfaithfulness, sin, wrong or bad decisions, character issues (self-inflicted storms). Then there are storms satan and his demons created to distract or discourage us, or just to keep us busy (demonic storms). And finally, there are storms that God orchestrated to teach us something valuable (God storms).

Understanding which kind of storm you are in will help you to navigate that storm. And knowing what the origin of the storm is can give you keys on how to remain standing during that storm and how to get through it. Part of this understanding comes from knowing who is speaking into your life.

What (and whom) are you listening to?

A storm can start suddenly and come crashing into your life, but it can also start subtly. Sometimes it will be like a thunderstorm that seems to have come out of nowhere, and before you know what is happening, you are in the middle of thunder, lightning and torrential rain. Other times, it will start with a little voice that speaks to you about your circumstances. For example: *No one is going to read your book. What does your voice even matter? You don't even have the money to pay your electricity bill. Look at the mess you have made of your life. How could you ever speak publicly? You hypocrite!* It is voices like these, subtle, quiet voices that you start to believe, that can be the start of a storm in your life. Storms in life and attacks from the enemy will always be on the horizon. But we can empower these storms and whispered lies from the enemy, or we can defuse them. That is our own choice and under our control. A small seed of unbelief can grow into a huge tree with destructive, poisonous fruit, but we can also prevent it from taking root in the first place. We do that by knowing God's Word. If a thought that crosses my mind is not in line with God's promises in His Word, then I should know that it is a seed of doubt that does not come from God.

Perhaps you are worried about something that God has spoken about, but you have no idea how you are going to pay for it. At the moment of writing this book, this is the year in which I will celebrate my twenty-fifth anniversary in fulltime ministry. After all these years, this is the number one thing I hear: *How are we going to pay for that? How are we going to afford that?* Nowhere in the Bible do I read that if God has spoken something over our lives, that we are expected to pay the bill. The Bible does not say that, or anything even remotely close to that. What it does say, and what He asks of us, it to remain standing in faith.

> Therefore put on the full armor of God, so that when the day of evil comes, you may be able to stand your ground, and after you have done everything, to stand.
> – EPHESIANS 6:13

You see, it is not a question of "if the day of evil comes", but "when the day of evil comes". Storms happen, so we need to know how to keep standing, and have faith in God.

Emotions are real but not leading

The first thing I think of, when I think of keeping the faith and standing on God's promises, is the song "Great is Thy faithfulness", or the song "Lord, You're so good". That is something I have learned from experience, that God really is good. In the despair, in the brokenness, His incredible goodness and faithfulness were there. I know that He is able to take the biggest mess, that which you think can never be made right, and fix it and bring complete restoration and healing.

A very important part in remaining standing in faith through the storm is to pay close attention to our words and what we say out loud. Yes, I do believe that God wants us to share our emotions with Him and tell Him how we are feeling, no matter how awful our feelings may be. There are moments in our life that we need to express those emotions, let them out, but know this: *They are not the truth!* Emotions are feelings, not truth. But His goodness, His faithfulness, that there is always a way out of the despair, the darkness, the nastiness—that is the truth and that is leading. That there is a peace available to us that will calm us in the midst of the most horrid storm, that is the truth. A peace that we cannot understand, that does not make sense to our minds. "And the peace of God, which transcends all understanding, will guard your hearts and your minds in Christ Jesus" (Phil. 4:7).

When there is a storm in our life, God can send His peace that is unfathomable. And when you think that God has forgotten you, when you feel abandoned and alone, it is then that He is holding you tight. The emotions that you feel at that moment are simply not true. When I was going through a storm, when things happened to me, I thought: "This is the truth." But our emotions lie to us. They lied to me. We should be led by His truth, not our emotions.

Watch what you say

What I have learned in my storms is to see the bigger picture. So the moment you are in a crisis, or in the middle of a storm, then it can seem like that is all there is. That your whole life is a crisis or a storm. Because of the pounding of rain, you cannot see ahead. Because of the wailing wind, you are deafened to other sounds. It can seem like there never was anything other than the storm, and worse yet, that there will never be anything else than that storm. But that storm, that crisis that you feel like you are drowning in, is but a small piece of a much bigger picture. It a small piece of a puzzle that, when complete, will form the most amazing and unimaginable picture. Though the storm may seem to last forever, it will end at the right time. God will pull you out of it so you do not drown. For me, if I had remained in the storm, then the calling that was on my life might have been broken by the storm.

Guard your heart against adopting a victim mentality

But because you are in the middle of the storm, because you are temporarily blinded and deafened, you cannot see where all of this is leading. For me, looking back on certain storms, I can see that they led me to a breakthrough that was exactly what I needed at the time. Afterwards it all seems so clear, but at the time of great turmoil, your emotions can get the better of you and you may say things you shouldn't. I really have learned to take responsibility for the things I have said, for the things I did wrong, or could have done better. That really helped me. Whether in public or in your personal life, if there are things that you have said or done that were not right, take responsibility for them. Do not hide behind the excuse: "Yes, but I was going through a demonic storm!" Or: "I was in the middle of a process and I was very upset!" Do not allow yourself to give in to a victim mentality; though you may be a victim at the time, taking on a victim mentality will cripple you. Yes, it is rough. Yes, it is hard. Yes, it may be the most painful thing you have ever experienced. Yes, you may even legitimately be a victim in all of this. But guard your heart against adopting a victim mentality. Once you start to feel, think, act and speak like a victim, you will actually victimize others.

So when you find yourself in the middle of a storm, or even just in day-to-day life, you can still choose which seeds you allow to take root. Will it be the seed of promises that God has given you, or the seed of unbelief? When you receive the promises of God and allow them to take root, then you can see what happens in the Bible:

> Those [seeds] on the rocky ground are the ones who receive the word with joy when they hear it, but they have no root. They believe for a while, but in the time of testing they fall away. The seed that fell among thorns stands for those who hear, but as they go on their way they are choked by life's worries, riches and pleasures, and they do not mature. But the seed on good soil stands for those with a noble and good heart, who hear the word, retain it, and by persevering produce a crop.
> – LUKE 8:13-15

The seeds of doubt from the enemy can fall on the soil of your heart if you allow them to. They too can take root. And both of those seeds will lead to words, words of life, or words of death. "The tongue has the power of life and death, and those who love it will eat its fruit" (Prov. 18:21). So watch what comes out of your mouth, watch what you say, and examine what seed is the source of your words.

What you don't realize now is that just around the corner of the tunnel is a great breakthrough and fulfillment of God's promise waiting for you, and the only way to get there is to keep walking, not giving up, not walking back or trying to find an emergency exit. There is simply no other way to see the fulfillment of God's promise in your life than to keep on walking through the storm. So stand firm. Keep the faith. Don't give up!

4

SELF-INFLICTED STORMS

Surviving what you
brought upon yourself

We all have gone through a self-inflicted storm in one way or another. We read about several men and women of God in the Bible who were walking in their calling and destiny and went through storms they created themselves. It's very important to discuss this, because I have seen people with an anointing and calling of God on their life create their own storm. These storms were caused by wrong decisions or sin and then they blamed God, rebuked the devil or judged others instead of taking responsibility for the storm their behavior and decisions created.

King David – the story of his life

In these storms you are the one who is responsible for the start of the storm and the consequences, and also the one who holds the key to make it stop. I want to take a look at the life of King David. We can clearly see four seasons in his life.

1. There was a prophetic word spoken over him, a promise from God (1 Sam. 16:1-13).
2. Several difficulties took place.
3. His character was formed by these same difficulties.
4. Now that his character was able to carry the weight of responsibility, the spoken word became manifest in the life of David and he was crowned king.

The greatest king in Israel's history was anointed as king at an early age. However, David did not actually become king until about fourteen years after he was anointed, and even that took place in phases. First, he was crowned king over Judah and seven years later he was crowned king over all of Israel. During this period of waiting, he faced some very difficult circumstances. He was rejected by the ruling king at the time, King Saul, forcing him into exile. And then later, while he was in hiding, he was rejected again. The second time it was by some of his own people. Even though he had saved them from the Philistines previously, and even rescued one of their towns, they decided to turn him over to Saul. He was forced to flee again. Other men who had also been rejected followed him, and those men, those rejects, would later become David's "Mighty men". But at the time they were unwanted, despised, fallen from grace, just like David.

After David and his band of followers had to go into complete exile, he and they befriended the people they had once conquered, the Philistines. But the Philistines did not trust him and kept him at a distance, eventually rejecting him too. It seemed like nobody wanted the future king of Israel, like the promise once spoken would not come into fulfillment.

Things just seemed to go from bad to worse for David and his mighty men. They had gone out to battle and when they returned to their home city, they discovered that it had been burned and ravaged in their absence. Their families were taken. Their homes were in ruins. They had nothing left. There was such despair that the mighty men started to talk about stoning David for what had happened. Even David's friends were about to abandon him. But David did something that would make him an example for Christians throughout the ages:

> David was greatly distressed because the men were talking of stoning him; each one was bitter in spirit because of his sons and daughters. *But David found strength in the LORD his God.*
> – 1 SAMUEL 30:6

Years later David finally became king over all of Israel. After a process of transformation that started when he received a prophetic word, the prophecy was finally fulfilled and he was walking in the fullness of his calling as the king over all of

Israel. He went from shepherd boy, forgotten in the fields, to one of the greatest kings of all time. He was the greatest army commander Israel had ever known, successfully leading his people into battle and conquering all their enemies. There was peace in the land like there had never been before. God's hand was clearly on David in everything that he did. But then, years later, there came a day when it was time to go to war and be on the frontline, and David decided to stay home and take it easy. Listen, if God has called you to go to war, to be on the frontline, then you better go, because if He calls you there, it is the safest place to be! King David chose to stay home when God said go, and instead sent out his army while he stayed back. What happened next is one of the most dramatic stories in all of the Old Testament.

> Some storms are caused by
> wrong decisions or sin

One night King David was on his rooftop in Jerusalem. He spotted a beautiful woman bathing. Her name was Bathsheba (2 Sam. 11:2). David asked his servants about her and they told him she was the wife of Uriah, one of David's mighty men. Despite her marital status, David used his power and influence and ordered Bathsheba to sleep with him in the palace. Under pressure, she did.

How to hide adultery?

Bathsheba later discovered she was pregnant, and she informed David. David's initial reaction was to try to hide his sin. He devised a plan and commanded Bathsheba's husband, Uriah, to come back from the battlefield. Uriah was a man of honor and immediately obeyed his king's command. David sent him home for some rest and relaxation, hoping that Uriah would sleep with Bathsheba and through that provide a cover for the pregnancy. However, instead of listening to David, Uriah slept in the palace servant's quarters. He could not bring himself to take time off and relax when his men were still at war on the battlefield. Uriah did the same thing the next night as well, even though David got him drunk that evening, showing integrity in sharp contrast to David's attitude. It became clear that David and Bathsheba's adultery could not be covered up that way. David was called a man of God, was respected and had a lot of influence, but David abused his leadership and influence to get his way and to follow his flesh and own desires.

David made a second, more awful plan. He commanded his military leader, Joab, to place Uriah on the frontline of battle and then to purposefully fall back from him, leaving Uriah exposed to enemy attack. Joab followed the order, and Uriah was killed in battle. After her time of mourning, Bathsheba married David and gave birth to a son. But 2 Samuel 11:27 says: "But the thing David had done displeased the LORD."

You are the man!

When David and Bathsheba's child was born, the Lord sent the prophet Nathan to confront David. Nathan used a story A rich man took a poor man's only ewe lamb and killed it, even though he had many flocks of his own. David, a former shepherd, was so angered by this story, which he thought was true, that he responded, "As surely as the LORD lives, the man who did this must die! He must pay for that lamb four times over, because he did such a thing and had no pity" (2 Sam. 12:5).

Nathan then pointed at David and spoke the words, "You are the man!" David was guilty of this sin, and judgment would be upon his house in the form of ongoing violence. David immediately repented and Nathan said, "The LORD has taken away your sin. You are not going to die. But because by doing this you have shown utter contempt for the LORD, the son born to you will die" (2 Sam. 12:13-14). The child died a week later, and David's household experienced further hardship in later years. In total, four of David's sons suffered untimely deaths—the "four times over" judgment David had pronounced upon himself.

Psalm 51 was written by David when the prophet Nathan came to him after David had committed adultery with Bathsheba.

> Create in me a pure heart, O God, and renew a steadfast spirit within me. Do not cast me from your presence or take your Holy Spirit from me. Restore to me the joy of your salvation and grant me a willing spirit, to sustain me. Then I will teach transgressors your ways, so that sinners will turn back to you. Deliver me from the guilt of bloodshed, O God, you who are God my Savior, and my tongue will sing of your righteousness. Open my lips, Lord, and my mouth will declare your praise.
> – PSALM 51:10-15

True repentance

David realizes that he has failed as king and leader. He acknowledges his sin, and shows true repentance the moment he was confronted with his sin. He was not sorry he was caught (as many are), but instead the first words out of his mouth were: "I have sinned against the LORD" (2 Sam. 12:13). He was in a storm of his own making; the turmoil in his life, the consequences for so many people around him, not in the least his own baby, were all as a result of his own actions. The key in David's storm, created by himself, was repentance, accepting the consequences and taking responsibility. Instead of giving up, he repented, knew he was forgiven and chose to keep walking in faith, embracing the calling of God on his life.

In the account of David and Bathsheba, we find several lessons.

1. Secret sin will be exposed.
2. God will forgive anyone who repents.
3. Sin's consequences remain even when the sin is forgiven.
4. God can work even in difficult situations.

In fact, David and Bathsheba's next son, Solomon, became the heir to the throne.

What if I have created my own storm?

What we can learn from the story of David is that it's possible to create a storm in your own life that rages in the lives of your family and others around you. It brings pain, fear, torment of soul, sleepless nights and sometimes overwhelming guilt when you realize what you have done. But know this, when you have truly repented before God and made things right with others as much as is possible, full restoration is possible. There is grace and forgiveness. David didn't stop being king because he had sinned. He found forgiveness and healing with the Lord.

If you want to see your self-inflicted storm come to an end, then you must stop doing what caused it in the first place. If you are living in sin, stop it. Don't continue out of some sense of it being too late, or you being too far gone, or that there is no more restoration possible. It is so easy, once you have become entangled in sin, to end up in a downward spiral, and to keep repeating what got you there in the first place.

You will need to humble yourself before the Lord. Tell Him where you have failed, where you have made wrong choices. Know that the moment you come before Him and confess your sin, you are already forgiven. The next step is taking responsibility for what you have done, *and* for the consequences of your actions. When your actions become public, there will be a moment in which you can choose to take responsibility for your actions, or to hide it as much as possible. See the thoughts "that it is not that bad", "everyone does this", "I am not hurting anyone", for what they are: Lies that will eventually destroy you and those around you. When you entertain those thoughts, you will remain in sin, remain in the destructive downward spiral. Instead, you must make a conscious choice to bring everything into the light, so the enemy has no more legal right to torment and destroy you.

Remember that even though David had committed several very serious sins, adultery and the murder of the husband of Bathsheba, God called him "a man after his own heart" (1 Sam. 13:14). Why? Because David knew what it was like to live from a place of brokenness. He wanted to have a clean and pure heart and always be in the presence of God. He knew that it was God who had made him king, that it was not his own achievements. He knew where he had come from, his humble beginnings as a shepherd boy who was rejected even by his own family. His utter reliance on God and His mercy, his desire to be near Him, is what set David apart.

The key to surviving your own storm and stopping the storm is taking responsibility for the mistakes or bad decisions you made. Start today by taking responsibility for the pain you have caused in this storm, and if you made bad financial decisions, take responsibility for that as well. Learn to be humble enough to say sorry and ask forgiveness and make a plan so that this will not happen again. Don't try to hide your mistakes, don't allow the enemy to find a way to attack you with hidden sin and issues, especially when you are on the frontline of the Kingdom of God.

The good news is that there is grace, forgiveness and full restoration in God's Kingdom if we are humble enough to admit our mistakes and take responsibility for them. Your part in this is to take responsibility for the things you have done that created this storm. Stop judging others, forgive yourself, seek help and do everything you can to make it right with the people who are hurt by the things you have done. Acknowledge that it is God who brought you through up until this point, and your need for His presence on a daily basis.

No more shame

Many people, once they realize what they have done, respond by feeling humiliated and ashamed. They believe the lies of the enemy about their identity and wallow in the shame of their sin and what they have done. The enemy will bring back all their sins of the past, even the ones they have confessed and made right with God and others. They mistakenly think that humbling themselves before the Lord is living a life of shame and punishing themselves over and over again. They think that "being poor in spirit" (Matt. 5:3) means *humiliation and shame*, not an attitude of *humility and brokenness*.

The key in David's storm was repentance, accepting the consequences and taking responsibility

---

David went to a place of brokenness, and through his brokenness there was repentance. The sin was not necessary for his brokenness. The place of brokenness is the place where we should live. This is not a place where we critique ourselves or others; that is not humility. Feeling bad about yourself is not humility. Any time we give room to a past sin which has already been forgiven by the blood of Jesus, we are guilty of false humility. It denies His forgiveness and His blood, so when you feel bad it does not mean you are humble.

When I am weak, He is strong (2 Cor. 12:10). I have caused many of my own storms in my life. I think the most important part when you are going through a storm that you have caused yourself, is to acknowledge that you caused it, instead of blaming other people. Take responsibility for what you have done and set things straight.

You can also make the wrong choices in a relationship, ending up in a storm. It may feel like all of the turmoil is coming out of nowhere; as if you are a victim of your circumstances, but you are not a victim. It was your wrong choices that got you there. You see, when we make choices based on emotions, based on the temporary "high", the feeling, then we often do not make the right choices, especially in relationships. Many times, in relationships, where most storms are experienced, these storms can be highly destructive. Yet these storms are not demonic, or only one person's fault. There are two people involved in a relationship, and two people responsible for the well-being of that relationship. Relationships that have not been blessed by God can be particularly problematic.

So how do you end the storms in a relationship? How you enter a process together, especially if you are married, is very important, and sometimes it is the leading cause of storms. Some people get married too quickly, or want to be together based on emotions or lust. They step into a relationship together, end up in bed together, have children, and form a life together without the right foundation. Then when storms come, no one wants to take the responsibility, or bear the consequences of their choices; that maybe this was not the life partner God had intended for them in the first place. So when you start to realize that you are in a storm that you have caused yourself, then taking responsibility starts with acknowledging that you made a wrong choice, or a choice that was not wise. And then what do you do? You turn to God. God's mercy, His supernatural intervention, is available to us. However, there are two parties involved and both have to be willing to submit to Him.

Taking offense

I think the biggest storms that people cause themselves

are started with assumptions. Assuming the other person understands you, or will do something for you, or will act in a specific manner. And then, when they do not fulfill your expectations, do not meet your assumptions, you are hurt and offended. Being offended can be very destructive, because when you are offended, you are operating from a place of being owed something. When a person does not fulfill your expectations, you are waiting there, offended, for them to do, say or give you something. They "owe" you. And when you hold on to that offense, digging your heels in as you wait for them to "make it right", the offense grows in your mind and becomes so big the other person can never make it right. It is never enough. Taking offense morphs into unforgiveness and bitterness. By not forgiving the other person, you start your way down a path of destruction.

We can all think of many examples, I am sure, of people around us. People who have taken offense by something we have said. Perhaps they had a certain expectation, or they are offended by the choices we have made. Maybe they could not be a part of the process and they start to view us through a lens of offense, clouded by their own pain. And we see how their emotions come from their own pain, which they then mirror to us. All of a sudden, they are in a storm of their own making.

We experienced this with someone we know. This person later told us that this is what they felt and experienced, and currently our relationship is completely restored. This person had taken offense because of some of the choices we had prayerfully made with the Lord as a family. We really felt like the Lord was leading us in a certain direction. And that person was offended. This caused a storm, a disrupted relationship, isolation, distance. The only way this storm could be resolved was for this person to realize that they had taken offense. The moment this person asked for forgiveness, love could flow once again. There was understanding, acceptance and restoration.

This is a problem that occurs all over the world, in every church. We are all quick to take offense, causing church splits and broken relationships. Relationships are broken, people no longer trust other people, all as a result of taking offense. Often, when we take offense, we say things out loud, voice our opinions of the other person, speaking things about another person that are not in line with God's Word.

Being offended can be very destructive

I too have been guilty of this. There was a person that I had become offended with, and I was no longer able to see them as a child of God, but rather viewed them as my enemy. Because suddenly that person is "against you". It starts out as something small, but if not dealt with, will become a huge storm. Yet you can end that storm. All you have to do is forgive. And you will see that when you speak out the words of forgiveness, that storm will disappear. Yes, it may take time for trust to be rebuilt, but it can be done and there is a way out of living in offense.

Going through a crisis or a storm we created ourselves can result in one of two things. Either we become hungry for more of Him, or we turn to things that distract us from Him. We shut down and play more games on our phones, or we start to binge-watch Netflix series, or we fill our "free" time with empty, worldly things. There is nothing wrong with playing games on our phones, or with watching Netflix. But if we spend more time with these things than with seeking God, then we will miss the point of why we are going through this season in the first place. If we do not grab the opportunity and start working on the changes that need to be made in our lives, then we will not learn our lesson and continue to go through storms like these again and again. This will happen until we learn to fill our hearts and minds with His promises, His Holy Spirit and His purifying fire.

Return to your first love

So let us return to the place where we are hungry for more of Him, just like it was when we first fell in love with Jesus. Let us cry out for more of the Holy Spirit, so that we can be cleansed by the holy fire that will burn away anything that shouldn't have been there in the first place.

Let's go back to the place where we can't stop reading the Word of God. Where we don't care about our belongings, fame or success, we are just hungry for more. To that place where we don't care about our reputation or other people's opinions. Where we don't worry about what people say or think about us. Yes, we still love people, but we do not need to accept their (negative) thoughts about us. As long as we are connected to Jesus and completely surrendered to Him, then He will speak out the truth over us. Love never required agreement with people who are not walking or living by faith. The baptism with fire will purify that which is truly important. You will see that certain things that were once important to you are no longer on your list when you have been baptized in fire. Suddenly everything has shifted in terms of priority.

We really need the fire baptism in the process, in the storm. It will create a clean heart, and renew our spirits. That is what will change the environment around you. Go to the secret place with God. The most wonderful thing you can do in crises and processes is to spend time with Him in the secret place and have an encounter with the Holy Spirit and the fire of God touching your lips, like He did with Isaiah (Isa. 6:5-7).

5

DEMONIC STORMS

When it feels like all hell
is breaking loose

The story of Job is probably one of the most well-known stories when it comes to demonic storms. It looks like Job lost everything he could possibly lose. As you read his story in the Bible, you can see he was a great leader, a man of integrity and one who was favored by God. Wealthy and blessed, Job took care of other people, the widows and the orphans. Job seemed to be a wonderful man of God, who was conscientious to the point of making sacrifices in case his children had perhaps sinned unawares (Job 1:5).

And then the most horrible, traumatic, demonic storms came into his life, and he lost nearly everything, except his faith and trust in God. Even though you are a believer, and lead a righteous life, it does not mean you will not experience storms or go through processes in your life. The storm in Job's life involved unimaginable grief, demonic pressure, physical pain and illness, and spiritual suffering. Job understood that the God whom he so faithfully had served, and the God who was powerful enough to stop all of this from happening, the God who could have prevented his suffering, allowed it to take place. God did not create the storm that Job went through, but He did allow it.

Faithful to the point of death

Job's wife was not much help. Actually, she was so angry at God for the losses they had experienced, she was sure that Job would be better off dead. I am sure she was hurting because she lost all of her children too. As a couple they lost their possessions, their children, and probably their standing in the community. Her lack of faith in a God who somehow allowed all of these horrible things to happen was very powerfully expressed as she saw Job suffering from horrific boils:

"Are you still maintaining your integrity? Curse God and die!" (Job 2:9). These words show that she had been pushed to breaking point as she would rather be a widow and live with the stigma attached to that, than be associated with the man who "obviously" must have sinned or none of all those things would have happened to him.

His close friends also tried to convince Job to blame God for everything he went through. And if God was not to be blamed, then it must be Job who had committed some horrible sin, otherwise he would not be experiencing all of these terrible things. Initially they seemed to support Job, sitting with him as he suffered. But after some time, they become convinced that he must have done something, because how else could you explain all of these awful things? People often look to blame someone when something bad happens. Either they blame God, or the person it happened to.

But Job stayed faithful. In his despair, pain, distress and anxiety, Job kept his faith in God and in His promises. "Though he slay me, yet will I hope in him; I will surely defend my ways to his face" (Job 13:15). Imagine going through all that Job went through, and continue to hope in God, even to the point of death by God's own hand. All of this distress and development of his character in walking through the storm in faith was rewarded in the end. Job received double blessings and many things were restored as a double portion. However, he did not know this during the storm.

Feeling like Job

My friend, if you have ever been betrayed, forsaken, cheated or hurt, you have experienced the trauma and pain at the heart of it all. You can understand where Job is in his life and what he is going through. Yes, we know and trust in God's words. We know that His Word tells us that He is in control and that He is a good Father. He promises to love us always and never leave us (Heb. 13:5). And yet He allows these things to happen.

When the demonic storm came crashing into Job's life, he was unmovable. The rain of sadness poured down on him as he suffered from painful sores all over his body. His heart was broken from the grief of losing his children. And yet, through this all, Job remained faithful to God. He was going through the most horrible time in his life, he was battered and bruised by a storm of physical, emotional and spiritual pain.

> In his despair, pain, distress
> and anxiety, Job kept his faith in God
> and in His promises

Dear reader, this could be where you are in your life right now, hurting, broken and bruised. You may be asking yourself why Good Father God allowed these things to happen to you. The storm you are facing may even be at breaking point, the point where you feel you are about to go down. You find yourself in the midst of the storm and you are wondering what is going to happen. I have often seen that when we do not understand why a storm is happening to us, and do not know what the source of the storm is, we cannot see what is waiting for us at the end of it. And when we have no vision of what it will be like when the storm ends, when we have no hope that things will get better or change, then it is very difficult to maintain our faith in God. This is the point where many people lose faith and walk away from God. That is why it is so important to discern which type of storm you are facing. Which leads us to the question: How do we discern whether what is happening to us is actually a demonic storm?

Discerning a storm's origins

Demonic storms often start with an accusation. Suddenly you are plagued by thoughts that are not in line with God's

Word. These thoughts and words are discouraging and heavy, like a burden. You sense a certain weight, an atmosphere that is not peaceful, and feel unrest and delay.

During a demonic attack you will notice that many things seem to be delayed. How is that possible? The financial provision that does not come in, though God spoke to you about it. Things you own break suddenly, finances are delayed, and when you pray it feels like the heavens are made of bronze (Deut. 28:23). When we look at the story of Daniel, we see that the angel Gabriel needed the archangel Michael's help in the battle to break the demonic resistance before he could get to Daniel. Delay is often a very clear sign that you are dealing with a demonic battle. And during that delay, you struggle to encourage yourself, it takes extra effort to read God's Word, and you start to doubt. You are under attack and doubt, fear and unbelief are part of the munition the enemy uses. And your circumstances would seem to confirm your doubts and unbelief. It is as if your circumstances are yelling at you, "See, I told you so! I just knew it was too good to be true!"

Another way to discern a storm's origins is that there are people who say things to you that normally would not speak like that. I have literally experienced that other Christians, children of God, would become enraged, under the influence of an insane anger, and say awful things. Their words are not in line with God's Word. That is a sure sign it is demonic.

When miscommunication occurs between a husband and wife, when it feels like you no longer understand each other, and you catch yourself viewing your partner as your enemy, pay attention! When it seems as though the atmosphere has changed, as if you cannot find each other, when there is no longer a connection, then know this: That is not of God and your partner is not your enemy. Instead, you are under attack.

Sudden illnesses are also a sign that you could be dealing with a demonic storm. Sickness never comes from God. The Bible says that Jesus took all of our sicknesses and diseases and our healing is in Him (Isa. 53:5).

Keys to breakthrough

It may be that you have a general sense that something is not right. You cannot exactly put into words what is wrong, but you just know something is off. When you do realize that you are going through a demonic storm, and you recognize the source of the storm, it is often a turning point. Recognizing it and asking God for the keys to breakthrough will bring victory. This may take a few days. You would think that once you have identified the source, and applied the keys that the Holy Spirit has shown you, that everything would be okay. But I have experienced that the breakthrough often takes time to appear. The breakthrough is also a process. And when you come out on the other side of the storm, you look back and wonder: "What on earth just happened?!"

We experienced this some time ago. God had spoken about the Olympic Stadium in Amsterdam, that it would be used as a historic location for several amazing events. The price to use the stadium is very high, and it is nearly impossible to hold any type of event there due to the many rules and permits needed. But God had spoken about this, so for a long time I did not doubt that we would be able to use the Olympic Stadium.

Then, just before I went to bed one night, I had had a conversation with someone. That person did not mean harm, nor did they realize that their words were demonically inspired. They said, "Yes, every year we organize a big day for Christian youth in the Netherlands. However, we cannot do that in the stadium anymore because there are just not enough visitors. These kinds of events are shrinking. That is why we are now using a smaller venue in a different location. What are you thinking, using the Olympic Stadium? You have invited speakers that 90 percent of the Dutch have never heard of, and those speakers have a vision that we don't know. The Christian organization Opwekking has been organizing events for forty years, and your organization is not even a year old. No one knows who you are, and now you want to use the Olympic Stadium? It's great that you have faith for that, but I don't see how this is going to happen."

Sleeping through the storm

There are two things you can do when confronted like that: One, you can believe it and let the doubt take over, or you can stand on God's promises once again. So the next morning I wrote down God's promise: "God has spoken about this and He will fulfil his promise. It is a beautiful promise." And yet, throughout the day that person's voice echoed in my mind and found a place to latch on and I started to believe what they had said. I thought, "Maybe I did not hear God's voice right, maybe this is not possible. What if we are there in an empty stadium, visible to the entire world, because it is going to be broadcast live all over the world?" These thoughts went on and on and dug deeper and deeper into my mind, until I could no longer sleep at night and I became so restless.

Asking God for the keys to breakthrough will bring victory

Due to my doubts and lack of faith I made room for the enemy. You see, satan brings storms into our life, and if we cooperate with him by having a lack of faith, and giving in to doubt and fear, then we make room for those storms. Satan will always show up with a storm in his wake, but Jesus had the gift of sleeping through the storm and He wants to bless us with that too. Look, we cannot prevent the storms from happening, because they will come. But we can learn to sleep through the storm.

That is what I want to learn. To be able to sleep through

the storm because I know that God has spoken. That even when the waves are crashing against my boat, I know: "We are heading to the other shore, because God has spoken." And these waves will help me to get to the other side, even though I don't like the waves. It's like a birth of a baby; there is no woman I know who enjoys contractions. In many cases contractions are painful (even though I do believe in painless delivery), but contractions have a purpose, and with every contraction you come closer to the breakthrough!

Using the keys God gives

My wife is a woman of great faith, and she stands by me. So when I was losing sleep due to what had been said about the stadium, she said to me, "Come on. We are going to take communion." It was the middle of the night and I said, "Do we need to do that now? It's late." But we decided to do it, and act in faith together. So down the stairs I went, in my bathrobe and wearing my slippers. I got the things ready for communion and brought them upstairs so we could take communion together. We broke the lies and doubt, and asked for the keys to the breakthrough. And you know what happened the next day? God gave us those keys. He told us how we could fill the stadium, how we could change certain things in the plan—only a week before, this would have been impossible. We later heard that one of our American partners had been under attack and unable to sleep too on the very same night, struggling with the same fears I had been struggling with.

Not only did my faith return as a result of that demonic attack, but also insights were gained about how to fill up the stadium; insights that we did not have prior to the attack. So though the attack was demonic, God still used it for his glory. The storm itself is aimed at paralyzing you, drowning you in waves of fear, and attacking your identity. However, the very moment you realize that something is off, that something does not feel right, that this is more than a natural fear, then the real culprit behind the storm is exposed. The storm will subside and disappear, as the demons cowardly slink away.

How a storm became a blessing

When we take another look at Job's life, we can learn so much. He went through terrible things, very painful circumstances, and yet, in spite of all that, he continued to trust God and stand on His Word. If we continue to stand on God's promises in faith when we are tested and everything seems to be terrible, by continuing to stand, the storm will become an amazing blessing.

> Therefore put on the full armor of God, so that when the day of evil comes, *you may be able to stand your ground, and after you have done everything, to stand.*
> – EPHESIANS 6:13

Pain and suffering are incredible tools that God can and does use to teach us and mold us. Going through pain and suffering changes people. Some become bitter, offended and angry, others are changed for the better and become more Godlike in character. What is the difference? Whether or not they continued to stand, after having done everything.

In the midst of the storm, Job met with God and he experienced the presence of God in the middle of his family trauma and the loss of his business. Because Job stayed faithful to God and did not give up, nor chose to partner with his group of unbelieving friends around him, we read in Job 42:12 how God "blessed Job's later life" even more than his earlier life. Remember that Job was already blessed before the storms hit his life. After the storm, after everything he went through, he was blessed more by God than prior to the storm. He lived another 140 years in greater blessing than before, and he saw his children, grandchildren, great-grandchildren and great-great grandchildren. The story of Job's incredible life closes with the following verse: "And so Job died, an old man and full of years" (Job 42:17). Job walked through the storm and remained standing, to go on to be blessed and live a full life.

Renting the Ahoy convention center

In the early years of my ministry, I was visiting my friends Bob and Kathy Fitts. While I was at the YWAM base in Kona, Hawaii, I saw many different flags from various nations. I felt led by God to gather people from many nations for an international event, and that I should rent the Ahoy Rotterdam convention center in the Netherlands to host this event. So we rented the Ahoy in Rotterdam, in faith. There are 10,000 seats in this convention center, and we had no real experience hosting such events at the time. We did not have a big team and there were few people who even knew about our ministry. It was through divine connections, orchestrated by God, that I was able to compile a list of international speakers who were willing to come to our event. At that time, many of these speakers had never even heard of me, but after seeking the Lord in prayer, they felt led to come. When I say international speakers, I am talking about very well-known Christian leaders. I was reading their books and admired them. That these leaders were willing to come was only through divine favor. You see, when God's wind blows in your sails, you will move forward with speed and favor, and many doors will be opened to you.

We had no money, but we had a word from God and a lot of faith. We signed the rental contract for the Ahoy. With just eight weeks to go, we decided to call the conference "Heaven on Earth". The start of the conference finally arrived and I remember being so overwhelmed by the pressure, the excitement, the blessings and the many challenges. There were more than 9,000 people from all over the world waiting in line. I will never forget that moment. To my right I saw an older gentleman, and I recognized him as Jan Sjoerd Pasterkamp, a general of the faith and a national leader in the Netherlands at the time. I wanted to go over and greet him. I had only recognized him from the times I had seen him speak at other conferences.

But on my way over to him, another leader, whom I did not know, came rushing up to me and he looked very upset and angry. He walked straight up to me and raised his voice, as he asked me how in the world I thought I could organize this conference without his permission. He said I was causing trouble. I was shaking as I asked him why. He said that he too was hosting a conference, at the same time and just thirty-five minutes' drive away from the Ahoy. The attendance at his conference was lower than expected because of the conference I had organized. He said that nobody knew who I was and that I would have to stop the conference. He walked away angrily.

I was left puzzled and confused, and I felt very rejected. I felt like I could cry at that moment. Things were already so overwhelming. Just then, pastor Jan Sjoerd walked up to me. He had seen and heard everything. He smiled at me, placed his arms around me and said, "Son, through what I just saw, I knew it was you in the prophecy. If you want me to, I am willing to help and support you as a spiritual mentor." I started to sob and asked him which prophecy he was talking about. Jan Sjoerd explained that he had received a prophecy from a well-known prophet, who stated that he would be a spiritual father and mentor for a young man in the Netherlands. This young man was tall, with blue eyes, and he would experience major resistance and pressure for some time because of his faith. Jan Sjoerd prayed about this after receiving the prophecy, and asked God who this young man could be. When he heard about the conference in Rotterdam, he felt led to go there a bit earlier. Then he saw what took place between this other leader who was so angry, and myself. He knew at that moment that I was the young man he was to help.

The storm itself is aimed at paralyzing you, drowning you in waves of fear

---

For many years Jan Sjoerd helped me in different processes and through storms. He was always protecting me, making me feel understood and heard. He took many proverbial bullets for me and protected me from many things. He became my spiritual father, mentor and one of the board members of our ministry. The angry outburst of this other leader, and the rejection I experienced, was used by God to highlight me to Jan Sjoerd, and opened the door for a wonderful relationship of many years. Today Jan Sjoerd is in heaven, but I will never forget him or what he did for me.

Heaven on earth

Thousands of people had a life-changing experience during that three-day conference. The presence of God was so incredible and many years later I still meet people who testify that their life was changed at that conference, how they met Jesus there and started to walk in their God-given calling.

After the conference, our ministry took off. Many blessings came our way and doors were opened for us. Along with those blessings a lot of criticism, judgment and curses also came our way. However, these things came from other Christians, not from unbelievers. You see, the moment you step into the prophetic word of God, when you start to do what God's Word says, you will face demonic opposition and storms.

Why? Because you take territory for the Kingdom of God. God's kingdom here on earth, as it is in heaven, does not come without a struggle. The moment you do anything that is connected to the building of God's Kingdom here on earth, reaching the lost, even one soul, then you take territory from the power and principalities of the darkness. They won't surrender without a fight. You must understand that building the Kingdom of God, expanding His Kingdom by bringing in lost souls, will be met with fierce opposition by the evil one. You will have to face and deal with these forces of darkness.

The Bible has a great example of the difference between how Jesus dealt with this demonic opposition and how the disciples dealt with it.

That day when evening came, he said to his disciples, "Let us go over to the other side." Leaving the crowd behind, they took him along, just as he was, in the boat. There were also other boats with him. A furious squall came up, and the waves broke over the boat, so that it was nearly swamped. Jesus was in the stern, sleeping on a cushion. The disciples woke him and said to him, "Teacher, don't you care if we drown?" He got up, rebuked the wind and said to the waves, "Quiet! Be still!" Then the wind died down and it was completely calm. He said to his disciples, "Why are you so afraid? Do you still have no faith?" They were terrified and asked each other, "Who is this? Even the wind and the waves obey him!"

They went across the lake to the region of the Gerasenes. When Jesus got out of the boat, a man with an impure spirit came from the tombs to meet him. This man lived in the tombs, and no one could bind him anymore, not even with a chain. For he had often been chained hand and foot, but he tore the chains apart and broke the irons on his feet. No one was strong enough to subdue him. Night and day among the tombs and in the hills he would cry out and cut himself with stones. When he saw Jesus from a distance, he ran and fell on his knees in front of him. He shouted at the top of his voice, "What do you want with me, Jesus, Son of the Most High God? In God's name don't torture me!" For Jesus had said to him, "Come out of this man, you impure spirit!" Then Jesus asked him, "What is your name?" "My name is Legion," he replied, "for we are many." And he begged Jesus again and again not to send them out of the area.

A large herd of pigs was feeding on the nearby hillside. The demons begged Jesus, "Send us among the pigs; allow us to go into them." He gave them permission, and the impure spirits came out and went into the pigs. The herd, about two thousand in number, rushed down the steep bank into the lake and were drowned. Those tending the pigs ran off and reported this in the town and countryside, and the people went out to see what had happened. When they came to Jesus, they saw the man who had been possessed by the legion of demons, sitting there, dressed and in his right mind; and they were afraid. Those who had seen it told the people what had happened to the demon-possessed man—and told about the pigs as well. Then the people began to plead with Jesus to leave their region. As Jesus was getting into the boat, the man who had been demon-possessed begged to go with him. Jesus did not let him, but said, "Go home to your own people and tell them how much the Lord has done for you, and how he has had mercy on you." So the man went away and began to tell in the Decapolis how much Jesus had done for him. And all the people were amazed.
– MARK 4:35-5:20

I want you to notice what Jesus said to his disciples. "Let us go over to the other side." He knew he was called to advance the Kingdom of God, that He had to cross over to the other side because there was a man tormented by the powers of hell, who needed his help. God had given Him territory. If God gives you territory, then there is always a season of crossing over. When Jesus crossed over to the other side, and set foot on the shore, He entered the territory of the Gerasenes. The people living there were pagans, not Jews. Jesus did not just enter a new geographical area, but also an area that did not belong to the Jewish nation, so it was a different spiritual territory too. The devil believed that the area of the Gerasenes belonged to him. It was not consecrated to God, unlike the nation of Israel. So Jesus knew He was entering a new territory.

New territory will lead you into storms

It is time for all of us to take new territory, to go beyond our cultural denominational borders. As sons and daughters, as the family of God, we are called to take new territory, and to seek souls that are lost. We need to tell the devil to back off, because we have the authority of Christ and are joining forces to advance the Kingdom of God. Are you a territory taker?

All storms are temporary

Just as Jesus stepped into new territory, crossing cultural barriers, seeking the one that was lost, the devil unleashed a storm in order to prevent Him from fulfilling His calling. When you preach the real gospel, you will provoke hell, and the demons will chase you and unleash a storm over you and your life. Your moving forward in faith causes a storm, and hell will try to get you to step back, or even better, give up, because storms are linked to taking territory. When Jesus crossed over to the other side, to the land of the Gerasenes, the devil and his demons knew that they would lose that territory to Jesus once He set foot on that shore. He would take that land for the Kingdom by saving a soul that was lost.

So when hell is chasing you, when the storms come over you, these are the attempt from the evil one to stop you, and Jesus in you, from setting foot on the other shore. That is why we go through church splits. That is why you have gone through fires, why you have gone through storms. It was hell chasing you, doing its best to get you to step back, or turn around, to stop contending for what God said is yours to take. If you have been through a storm connected to territory, it should awaken your spirit, because that storm was the sign that you were about to take some new territory, that God is about to give you the increase and the anointing for the harvest.

Don't give in to fear

When you are going through a demonic storm, do not give in to fear and unbelief. When the disciples were with Jesus in the boat and the storm roared through their lives, they were terrified. They did not understand that it is Jesus who has the authority over the wind and the waves. The same applies to us. When the storm is raging, the wind is howling and the waves are so high we feel we might drown, the fear and anxiety can be overwhelming. Just remember that Jesus knew who He was. The disciples did not. In this testing they had to learn who they were in Him, and what their response should be when they were facing demonic storms.

To get through this type of storm, it is important to know that it *is* a demonic storm. That it is the enemy trying to stop you from entering your promise, from taking your territory, from progressing to your next chapter in life, from doing what you were called to do.

You must remember the promises God gave you. And remember that all storms are temporary. Do not remain in the storm voluntarily, but keep standing until you get through it. Keep your eyes fixed on Jesus, He is your strength. Even though everything seems to be falling apart during the storm, there is a promise waiting for you on the other shore. And Jesus is there with you through it all.

> Though the fig tree does not bud and there are no grapes on the vines, though the olive crop fails and the fields produce no food, though there are no sheep in the pen and no cattle in the stalls, yet I will rejoice in the LORD, I will be joyful in God my Savior. The Sovereign LORD is my strength; he makes my feet like the feet of a deer, he enables me to tread on the heights.
> — HABAKKUK 3:17-19

6

GOD STORMS AND THE PITFALL OF REJECTIONS

How to deal with rejection
in the storm

This is the kind of storm that most Christians find difficult to understand. Sure, we can deal with storms that come as a result of our own mistakes or bad choices. We may even be able to identify with Job to a certain extent, as we see that the enemy is out to prevent us from reaching our calling. But when it comes to what I call "God Storms" and the rejection that we experience when we go through these, well, that is something else.

You have received a call from God, you just know you were made for it, and yet you are in a season in your life when quite the opposite is happening. Suddenly you are betrayed by someone close, you experience rejection, you feel wounded and broken. You feel like God is silent and distant, and not at all interested in you. You see, a God storm that He allows to take place can be a long process, one that He wants you to go through. This storm will not end until He says it ends. The most important thing to do during this time is to pray, praise, persevere and keep walking (not running)! The problem is that we often don't even recognize the storm as being a God storm. We cannot understand the purpose behind these God-ordained storms, so instead we blame the devil, ourselves or others, without understanding why God would allow certain storms in our lives. These storms always serve to bring us into our destiny! I want to take you on a journey through just such a storm. I promise you, by the time you are done with this book, you will start to understand certain things that you have gone through, and *why* you went through them. And when you do, it can lead to the breakthrough that you have been longing for so long.

Jesus was under attack

We have probably all read the portion of Scripture where Jesus was led into the wilderness by the Holy Spirit. It was there that He was tempted by the devil. When Jesus was hungry and thirsty, after having fasted for forty days, the devil came to attack Jesus. But Jesus did not allow Himself to be led by emotions when He responded to the attack; instead, His every word and action was led by the Holy Spirit. His temptation took place directly after He had been baptized by his cousin John the Baptist. A dove descended from heaven and a voice was heard stating: This is my Son, whom I love; with him I am well pleased" (Matt. 3:17). The very next verse says "Then Jesus was led by the Spirit into the wilderness to be tempted by the devil" (Matt. 4:1).

A God storm will not end until He says so

Jesus was led there by the Holy Spirit. He did not end up in the wilderness because of his own actions. Nor was it the devil who decided to isolate Him and attack Him. No, it was His own Father who led Jesus into this time of testing. It was God who, through the power of His Holy Spirit, sent Jesus into the desert, into the Garden of Gethsemane and ultimately, to the cross. We can see that directly after Jesus' public recognition, He was led away into the wilderness. The same applies to us; often after we have been placed in a new position or we have been publicly recognized, a storm will follow. And though Jesus had feelings and emotions just like us, though He had a physical body that was weak from lack of food, just like us, He did not allow His emotions nor His physical desires to lead Him. Instead, He defeated the devil with God's Word! Three times He was faced with overwhelming temptations, and three times He responded by saying: "It is written…"

Know the Word!

When we study this part carefully, then we can see that when God does bring storms into our lives, when His Spirit does lead us into a wilderness period and we are tempted to give up, we can look to Jesus as an example. There is not a wilderness nor temptation that He is not familiar with.

> For we do not have a high priest who is unable to empathize with our weaknesses, but we have one who has been tempted in every way, just as we are—yet he did not sin.
> – HEBREWS 4:15

When Jesus was tempted, He used His knowledge of God's Word as a defense. He was hungry and tired, isolated and lonely out there in the wilderness. But He did not allow Himself to be (mis)led by His feelings. He used God's Word. The devil will come to attack us in our wilderness, in our times of isolation and weakness. But we too can defeat him, just like Jesus did, by knowing God's Word. We must be able to say: "It is written ..." We must know God's Word and be able to find the verses that are applicable to our situation. We can confidently say: "By the blood of the Lamb and the word of my testimony: satan, you have no right to attack me. I will not bow to you. I will bow only to Jesus." Because God's Word clearly states that "They triumphed over him [satan] by the blood of the Lamb and by the word of their testimony" (Rev. 12:11). Know the Word! It is your protection and the ultimate weapon.

Attacking your identity is a key tactic

We have seen how Jesus used the Word of God as a weapon of defense against the attacks of satan. But how do you know something is an attack from the enemy, and not your own emotions or something else? The key tactic the enemy uses is attacking your identity. In many cases the enemy will cause people to question your integrity. That is how he attacked Jesus too. He attacked Jesus' identity and His inheritance. But Jesus already knew who He was in the Father and what His rights were.

When it comes to spiritual warfare, it is not about how big the attack is. Attacks on your identity are often quite subtle. You have to know who you are in Christ and what your rights are. Your rights are in Jesus, as He took your place and you are now in His place. "God made him who had no sin to be sin for us, so that in him we might become the righteousness of God" (2 Cor. 5:21). Because you are now in Jesus, you have the right to send satan away through the power of the blood of Jesus. You are now a son or daughter of the Most High God, *Abba* Father, and you are seated in the heavenly realms with Jesus. "And God raised us up with Christ and seated us with him in the heavenly realms in Christ Jesus" (Eph. 2:6). So when the enemy comes and attacks your identity, make sure you understand what your identity and your inheritance is. This is an important tool to defend against a key tactic of the evil one.

Heavily pregnant and riding a donkey

Jesus was not the only one to go through a God storm. Joseph and Mary also went through a stormy period, of which every step was directed by God. They had to travel from Nazareth—where Mary had heard from the angel that she was to be the mother of the Savior of the world—to Bethlehem for a census of the population. By the time Joseph and Mary were forced to travel, due to a decree by heathen rulers who did not serve God, Mary was heavily pregnant. When you are nearing your due date, everything becomes uncomfortable. It was no different for Mary. Joseph was forced into a situation, a storm, that was not of his own making. He had to find a way to get his heavily pregnant wife all the way from Nazareth to Bethlehem. According to Christian tradition, he decided to have Mary ride on the back of a donkey, while he walked along beside her. It was a very long journey to take on foot, and riding a donkey. Scholars estimate it took about seven days to travel the ninety miles.

Heavily pregnant and seated on the back of a donkey, there is no way that was comfortable! Mary was so far along in the pregnancy that the baby had probably already descended into the pre-birth position. She was pregnant with a promise. She was chosen by God, blessed, and there was great favor on her. However, during those seven long days on the back of a donkey, on the road to Bethlehem, she probably did not feel very blessed, chosen or favored. There was no visible sign that this pregnancy was a beautiful promise.

These storms always serve to bring us into our destiny

I am sure Joseph and Mary tried to make sense of their situation, which seemed to be the opposite of what God had promised. Perhaps if we were in their situation, we would be rebuking the evil spirits behind those Roman occupiers who had decreed such a stupid thing in the first place. Maybe you are in such a situation now. There is a promise on your life, beautiful words have been spoken over you, but the opposite is happening and you are feeling *very* uncomfortable. You know that like Mary you are highly favored, but you don't feel highly favored because of the circumstances. It can be hard to understand what is going on when you are in the middle of a seven-day journey on the back of a donkey.

Men are naturally solution-focused
Most men are wired in such a way that when a problem is presented, they will immediately look for a solution. This often

happens in relationships. When a woman shares something about a problem she is struggling with, then the natural tendency for her husband is to find a solution for that problem. When my wife shares a problem with me, then everything in me wants to find a solution for that problem right away, whereas all she needs is for me to listen to her. I have had to learn that what she needs first and foremost is comfort, someone to listen to her, and not necessarily for me to come swooping in with a way to fix the problem.

So Joseph did what he could to fix the problem they were facing. He put Mary on a donkey to make the long journey as comfortable as possible for her, even though they were expecting a baby to be born any day. He could not see the baby, and he knew it was not even his own child. And now they were on a long journey, not because they wanted to, but because they were forced to. He could not fix that problem for Mary. And when men cannot fix a problem, their natural response is to become frustrated or angry. So there they are. Joseph has promised to care for Mary, Mary who is carrying a promise. The Bible does not say that God spoke to them as they journeyed, so we can assume that heaven was silent during this trip. Imagine walking for seven days next to a donkey with your heavily pregnant wife riding it. How long do you keep walking with only a promise to hang on to?

After having walked for seven days they could finally see an inn in the distance. This was the solution to their problem! After such a long journey on foot over dusty roads, they were smelly, dirty, hungry and I am sure they were sore all over. Mary was that much closer to giving birth. She might have already been having contractions at that point. However, the solution was within reach—an inn. No, there was no jacuzzi, but there would be a clean bed, water, warm food and above all, peace and quiet. Now everything would be okay. Joseph knew that Mary could give birth at any moment, and that they had little time to spare. Ready or not, if they did not hurry, that baby was going to come. And if they did not get to the inn on time, she might give birth by the side of the road! Thankfully they did make it to the inn.

Have you ever given God a deadline? You know that a promise is about to be fulfilled, so you set a deadline in which you expect a solution or a breakthrough. But then it does not happen as you expected. What does that do to your faith in God, and in the promise that you received?

Whether or not they would arrive at the inn on time, that baby would be born sooner or later. Whether or not a financial gift arrives on time, that bill needs to be paid. Whether or not a new home is available on time, we will need to leave this house before a certain date. And whether or not I have found a new job on time, this job is over. And then what?

The solution was not in the inn

When Joseph knocked on the door of the inn, the door that he thought would bring a solution, it was the only thing he could think of that would help Mary as she carried the promise and blessing. This baby was promised by God, He was God's blessing for humankind, so surely God would take care of them, right?

Just like Mary's pregnancy, our promise can be a burden. Before we can embrace that promise, we need to go through pregnancy and birth. Sometimes it can seem like the promise on our life is more of a burden than a blessing for a season. However, God is allowing this situation, this season, this storm to take place, as it is preparing us for the next level, so you can live in the fullness of His Word and the calling on our life.

Joseph knocked and the door was opened, but he was not allowed to enter the inn, which would have been the perfect solution for them. "There is no room for you here." And the door was closed. Joseph's faith was tested and his character was developed in this process. This is the point where most people would give up because they would become so frustrated. Joseph, as a man, wanted to solve this problem, but now that was impossible. It seemed like they were not yet at the point where God wanted them to be. Do you think that Joseph and Mary viewed this as God's provision? Did they see how God as a loving Father was caring for them when the door to the inn was closed?

You will never discover the open door
of your promise until you have dealt with the
closed doors in your life

How many times do we find ourselves wondering the same thing? We have the promise, we are at the point of breakthrough, and then suddenly something goes wrong, a bump in the road, the door is closed and it now seems impossible for that promise to ever be fulfilled.

Rejection

We don't know how Joseph responded when the innkeeper told him there was no room in the inn. The Bible does not say that Joseph wanted to fight back, but I can imagine that he was angry and upset, and felt rejected. I think this was the point at which Joseph was bitterly disappointed. An avalanche of emotions rolled over him—depression, fear and doubt. His self-confidence was shattered. The solution he had envisioned had disappeared before his very eyes. Now what were they going to do?

I can imagine that Joseph was angry, simply because this is often the first emotion that a man feels when he is hurt and feeling rejected. He and Mary had already been on the road for seven days, Mary was about to give birth, there was no time to look for another solution, and now the door to the inn, the only solution there, was closed. Joseph had to go tell Mary that the door was closed, that there was no room for them in the inn, that she could not give birth in the safety and warmth of the inn. It is one thing to be rejected by one of several options, but to be rejected by your only option, your only solution for your problem, that really hurts. You really needed that job, that chance. You really needed love, help, comfort, encouragement and affirmation. You believed God, but now you are in a situation and you don't see a way out anymore. You also feel like you don't have the time to learn yet another lesson from the Lord. You need a breakthrough and you need it *now*.

Do you recognize this in your own life? Maybe you really needed a job, the interview went well, you were one of the final candidates, and yet they chose someone else. You didn't get the job. Yet you felt like this was the job for you, the one that was going to open doors for you. How are you going to go home and tell the children that there won't be enough money for groceries, or there won't be a summer vacation, or no presents for Christmas? Let me tell you a little more about rejection, the kind of rejection that goes even deeper. Not the rejection in and of itself, but the consequences of that rejection. I know the emotions of rejection all too well, that feeling in the pit of your stomach, what those emotions then do to your body. I know the thoughts that can swirl through your mind, how you may act and what words are said when a door is closed. But you will never discover the open door of your promise until you have dealt with the closed doors in your life.

7

HOPE IS THE KEY

It's all a matter of perspective

We can learn from Joseph and Mary's story that there is an opportunity, not in the door that may be open, but in the door that is closed. The reason why I say this is because you will never discover the open door of your promise until you have dealt with the closed doors in your life. You need to first deal with the rejection of the closed door, and not take it personally. Because it isn't personal, just like it wasn't in the story of Joseph. In his case it was simply because other people had arrived there before they did. It had nothing to do with whether or not he was suitable, or whether or not he had done something wrong. In the same way we should not view closed doors as personal rejection, as if we are not worth it.

Joseph had to go report back to Mary, and tell her they needed to keep on looking, though they did not know where to go from there. They had envisioned something very different for their life together before the angel had appeared to Mary. And now once again, what they had envisioned about the birth of their child did not look anything like the reality they were in at that moment. They were ready for the birth of Jesus, the promise, and everything they thought was going to happen fell apart.

Death and life are often intertwined. On the one hand something new is born, and on the other hand there is death and a form of rejection and destruction. It feels very contradictory: I should be happy, but I am struggling with fear right now. Happy with the blessing of a new baby, but angry because of the rejection. You are angry at the innkeeper, angry at God. Couldn't He have arranged for a place in the inn? You are doing his will; can't you count on Him to take care of you?

As Joseph and Mary kept on looking, they saw something else. It certainly was not a five-star luxury resort with soft pillows, an elevator, clean toilets and room service. That would

be the least you would expect to have when welcoming the
King of kings into the world ... but this wasn't a resort, it was
totally different.

The bread of life

That night Jesus was born. We think that He was placed in
a manger used for fodder for the feeding of animals, based on
the many images and songs about his birth. He, who was to
later state that He was "the bread of life" was placed in a manger, a source for food (John 6:35). This was just one of the many
prophecies that was fulfilled in Jesus' life. The place He was
born was also prophesied (Mic. 5:2; Num. 24:17). The shepherds
who came to see Him were tough men, used to fighting off lions
and bears and protecting their flocks from many dangers, just
like King David had done many years prior in the same fields.
As shepherds they protected the Good Shepherd, keeping the
place of his birth safe. Safe enough to be vulnerable, to give
birth to the promise. The shepherds who kept the sheep and
lambs safe were there to care for the Lamb of God.

While Joseph and Mary were still on their way, when the
door of the inn was closed, it may have seemed as though
God was not speaking, as if all was silent. But God had spoken to the wise men, who were already on their way before
Jesus was even born. The wise men came bringing myrrh,
frankincense and gold. Many scholars say that the gifts presented by the wise men to Jesus were enough to sustain his
family for a long time. If Joseph and Mary had not been in the
place where God had sent the wise men, then they would not
have received the provision they needed for the next season
(Ps. 72:10-11). If they had not been rejected by the inn, then they
would not have been in the place that had been prophesied
hundreds of years prior. It is hard to believe when you are in a
process, heavily pregnant and having traveled for seven days
on a donkey, that there will be wise men waiting on the other

side, carrying the provision and blessing needed for the years
to come. But dear friend, the wise men are waiting just around
the corner for you too.

Don't view closed doors as personal rejection

By the way, do you see the significance in this? Mary
was riding a donkey, she and Joseph were rejected and not sure
where to go. But once the promise had arrived, the provision
for the promise came riding in on camels. Perhaps the lesson
in all this is that we need to have experienced enough rejection
in order to be in the place where God's provision is waiting for
us. If I had been worried about my own comfort, then I would
not have been in the place where God was sending the wise
men with the provision. If Joseph and Mary had not been in
the stable, then they might have missed the wise men.

Giving up

I can truly identify with Joseph and how he responded.
Receiving a promise, and then moving forward in faith after
God had spoken, but going through the entire process in
silence. And in that silence we imagine what the breakthrough we need must look like. Then we reach a point at
which we see that our own plan does not work, and we experience rejection and closed doors when we try to make our
own plans and ideas work anyway. This is the point in which
people we know, people of whom it is obvious there is a calling
on their lives, give up, become frustrated, disappointed, angry
and bitter. They become angry at God, at the people around
them, they blame everyone else and sometimes they even
quit their ministry, leave their church and give up the call of
God on their life.

How we deal with rejection is the test that shows that we

can deal with what God has for us on the next level. It is of vital importance that we learn how to deal with "No" and with rejection. We are in good company, though. He who would be defined by rejection was already rejected prior to his birth. When we follow Him, then it makes sense that we too will experience rejection. The rejection we go through is part of our calling as Christians.

What do you do when you are doing God's will and it seems like God is not helping you? What do you do when you are doing God's will and the doors are slammed in your face? What you thought would happen, did not. But ... you see the stable up ahead. Though you have been through rejection upon rejection, the Holy Spirit says that there is provision and breakthrough on your horizon. It has been a long journey, a difficult process, a storm of not knowing and unfulfilled expectations, but now you can see something up ahead. You have cried, you have experienced pain, but something is visible on the horizon. The stable, where your promise is going to be born, is just ahead. It may not look like what you had imagined, but it is the place where your promise will be born.

You may need to let go of your own ideas at this point. You may need to release your feelings of spiritual superiority, of being better than those around you, especially when you have been a leader of a successful ministry for a while, or have been elevated by other people. You might have even been a unwilling Christian superstar in the eyes of other people and even though you don't want to be, it can give you a feeling of superiority. What you had in mind does not need to be the same as what God has in mind, but God would not have brought you here if He did not have a plan for you!

Being grateful in the midst of rejection

We can learn from this that it is important to be grateful when confronted with rejection. Every time you are dealing with some form of rejection, then that is a sign pointing in a direction. Everyone is happy when God opens a door, but we also need to learn to be thankful and shout "hallelujah" when He closes a door, because every time He closes a door He is saying, "It is not here, not now. I have a different place for you."

Whatever your rejection may look like, whatever form it may take, I want to ask you, dear friend, to find a way to praise Jesus in your situation and take time every day to be grateful. Thank God for those who rejected you, wounded and betrayed you, because the wise men are on their way with blessings and provision. It was good they rejected you, it was good that the door did not open, that you did not get that job, that it did not happen the way you thought it would; it was even good that you did not get that house.

I want to ask to you to find a place where you can worship Jesus the next time you feel rejected. Even if it is just for five minutes, just walk away from where you are at that moment and go to the bathroom, or head outside and just start to praise Jesus. Do not allow negative feelings to overshadow you, and watch what you say. Use your tongue to praise Him. Do this in faith, because how you feel is not what this is about. When you are dealing with rejection, then you feel awful. But you are not your feelings and you need to make a conscious choice to start to praise Jesus in the midst of your rejection. Praise Him until the Spirit of God takes over and He will start to build a wall of defense around your mind, to protect you from the stream of negative thoughts (and what other people who are not part of your process say in gossip and judgment). When you do this, the enemy flees; demons and dark forces cannot latch onto a thankful heart or onto a life that is anointed and dedicated to following Jesus and persistent in faith throughout the process and the storm.

Jesus experienced rejection too

Why was Jesus rejected? Do you know why? Why was the life of Jesus characterized by rejection? Why would He leave His throne in heaven where He was loved and worshiped, respected and honored, and come to earth where the majority of the time He would not be loved or worshiped? On the contrary, He would be hated, humiliated, ridiculed, beaten, wounded, dishonored, despised, rejected and even killed. There is only one, simple, glorious reason: Jesus was temporarily rejected so that we would be eternally accepted.

When we are dealing with rejection from the world, we can always look to Jesus, who was accepted by His Father. There is no level of rejection in our lives that we have been through or will go through that Jesus cannot identify with and that He did not experience. He knows. He knows about all of it, and He did not give up. Actually, in the life of Jesus it was the case that most of His rejection led to a breakthrough and a fulfillment of His purpose here on earth. Jesus was rejected by people, and even by God Himself at one point, so that we could be accepted by God as beloved sons and daughters.

God the Son, Jesus, came to humankind in human form, so that He could identify with us and save us from the state we were in, and the rejection that is the core of our broken humanity. We rejected God. When sin became part of humanity, it turned our hearts into sources of evil. "The LORD saw how great the wickedness of the human race had become on the earth, and that every inclination of the thoughts of the human heart was only evil all the time" (Gen. 6:5). We rejected the God who had created us, we rejected His rulership over us and set ourselves up as our own gods. And yet Jesus chose to subject Himself to our rejection, so that He could bring us acceptance.

Betrayal—the ultimate form of rejection

I want to tell you something about betrayal and the rejection connected to it. We don't like this topic, but it is so powerful and it can make us or break us. It is not uncommon, all of us have experienced rejection or will experience it at some point in our lives to a greater or lesser extent. It takes on various forms and we need to know how to deal with it. If we don't deal with rejection, then eventually we will not be able to lead the life that God has for us, because we will be bitter, angry and frustrated.

Jesus dealt with the most serious form of rejection. He knew why He was experiencing rejection. He was able to forgive those who betrayed and rejected Him and focus on His Father, on His love for people and His calling and purpose. After everything that Jesus went through, He could have confronted Peter after He had risen from the dead and said, "Why did you deny me, Peter?" He could have complained about how horribly He had been treated by the soldiers, how the religious leaders hurt Him and betrayed Him, how disappointed He was in Pilate who chose to free a criminal and did not listen to Him but to the opinion of the bloodthirsty crowds. But we do not read any of that, all we read is about how much Jesus loved Peter, the one who denied Him. Jesus asked Peter three times: "Peter, do you love me?" (John 21:15-25). He asked him that three times, for the three times Peter denied Him—denial being a form of betrayal. And Jesus' question was so filled with love for Peter that Peter felt His love in the core of his being. Then Jesus told Peter he was ready for his ministry, by telling him to feed His lambs and sheep, and to care for them. Peter was to be the rock on which the Church of Jesus would be built and the gates of hell would not overcome the Church (Matt 16:18). Jesus' response to the ultimate form of rejection, betrayal by someone He loved, was to forgive and promote him.

What is the fruit?

You see, it is not just about how we walk through our process and storm, and how our character is formed during that process, but it is the testing of our faith and the fruit we show after the storm has calmed down. The fruit will show if we have truly gone through the process, truly laid down our rights and learned to be humble, with a servant spirit and willingness to readily forgive. What comes out of our hearts and mouths after the process and the storm of betrayal and rejection, after having been wounded and deeply hurt, shows the fruit of what has been done in our hearts and how it has formed our character so we become more like Him. These are not things you can learn from a book, or when you are on a mountaintop, or at a Bible school, a Christian conference, or a Sunday church service.

As I mentioned earlier, it's so important to be grateful in the midst of rejection. When you go through a valley, a season and process of shadows, conflicts and pressure, when you feel rejected by the people you love and whom you care about, it is of the greatest importance that you are rooted and grounded in the Lord. All of the praise or criticism by other people will not matter much to you when you strengthen yourself in the Lord, when you are fully dependent on Him for everything you think, feel and do. When there is no one else around you, start to praise God and express your gratefulness, even though you may not feel like doing it.

Remember that this season is not (just) about your feelings, though they are real and even valid. Your feelings and emotions originate from your soul, and they are present and even important, so do not ignore them. However, do not let these emotions and feelings guide you, because they can be misleading. It is important to allow yourself to be led by your spirit, which is in close cooperation with the Holy Spirit, instead of being led by your soul. This is one reason why it is so important that you actively receive the Holy Spirit and invite Him in your life.

A good way to focus on praise and thankfulness, and to not get caught up in your emotions, is to write down everything you are thankful for. Or you can turn on some worship music:

YouTube is full of anointed worship that is focused on the presence of God. It is not important whether you feel like it or not, or what you feel, make a choice to start with worship. Another thing you can do is meditate on the promises of God. The Bible is full of God's promises, especially in the Psalms. You can also go over all of the prophetic words, visions and dreams that you have received or that have been spoken over your life. That is why it is so important to always write down what you have received. In the back of this book I have included a list of faith proclamations. You can use these to get started.

Hope is the key

I want to tell you that what you were made for is waiting for you when you come out of this God storm. In order to do what you were made for, you need a change of heart, a deeper level of trusting God, learning to build on Him when things are out of your control, things that you cannot explain. Trust Him in those moments, because that will help you when it feels like you are moving backwards and this storm will never end.

Everyone goes through storms in their lives. However, we Christians have an advantage that we have the guidance and comfort, as well as the fire of the Holy Spirit, to light our way and to burn away those things that do not belong in our character. Truly it is the hope we have through the Holy Spirit that is probably the most important key to get through the storms.

Have you ever ended up in a situation in which you had to deal with something that you did not start yourself, but it was as if it just fell on top of you and now you find yourself responsible for a situation that you did not ask for, but you have to act now to take care of it? I have experienced this several times, after having received a word from the Lord, but in the next season I ended up in a process of which I thought, "Lord, You have given me this promise and this word, so please walk with me through this process." But during the process it did not feel as though God was speaking to me, or that He was even with me. Of course I knew in my mind and my spirit that He was with me, but it felt as though I was walking through that process alone. Sure, I had family and friends around me for a period during that process, but it still felt as if I was going through it alone. It felt as if I had run out of time and I needed a solution *now*.

Some of you reading this will know exactly what I am talking about—the feeling as though there is no more time left. You feel immense pressure because there is a deadline for a very challenging situation and you need a breakthrough, an answer, and you need it now. During the process you thought you had a solution in sight, and you have fixed your hope on that solution, and you reach that solution at the same time as you have reached your breaking point, and then the door to that solution closes. There is no room in the inn, the door is shut, and all hope feels lost. You feel rejected by the innkeeper, by God, and you don't want to tell the people around you, but it feels like everything is falling apart. There is no more solution in sight, no more hope.

Have you been there? You have put all your hope on something, you had to fight to get to that point, but now that you are there, the door suddenly closes. When this happens, and the door shuts in our faces, a lie can sneak in. This lie whispers as if it was our own thought, "I am disqualified. I am not good enough. God does not care about me." This is a crisis, and every negative thing ever said to you can come bubbling up, and that track is put on repeat in our minds. Our best plan didn't work, that what we hoped didn't occur.

Rejection sensitive dysphoria

When you have been rejected, you recognize these emotions and feelings of hopelessness. This is what happens to your soul when you have been rejected. Rejected by a loved one, a leader, a friend or a family member, by the people who are closest to you, your employees, your board, your church, your school, your employer, colleagues, or even your own parents. Being rejected feels terrible. Some people are less sensitive to rejection than others, but there is a group of people that are extremely sensitive to rejection. I want to take a moment to explain this because for these individuals, and maybe that's you, the process of dealing with rejection takes on a whole other level.

Any type of rejection is a sign pointing in a direction

This group of people often also struggle with attention deficit hyperactivity disorder (ADHD) and there is a connection between ADHD and a hypersensitivity to rejection. They often lack the lens to filter rejection. This is also known as RSD, rejection sensitive dysphoria. Those who suffer from RSD have an extreme response to rejection. Most of us don't like rejection, but for this group of people, rejection is almost unbearable. Those with RSD can be traumatized by rejection to such an extent that it does something deep inside of them; it plays with them, tortures them, talks to them and keeps repeating in their mind day and night. It keeps them awake at night and causes them to lash out at those they love, hurting them. For those with RSD, rejection is unbearable. The pain is so deep. It can make you want to stay in bed forever. You stop trying to connect with people because there is such a fear of being or feeling rejected. People with RSD may do well for a while, but then something happens that triggers the RSD. When it is triggered, they go into this painful, dark, bitter, empty angry place.

In that place they don't hear, "I don't like your hair or your shoes", they hear, "You are ugly and stupid and you don't belong."

They don't hear their board say, "We don't like the way you responded to that email", instead they hear, "You are disqualified and we don't like you." RSD magnifies the rejection and makes it so much louder. The torment of rejection is so intense that some people commit suicide because the pain is unbearable. It seems like many people do not understand the dark place they are in. When you get rejected and have RSD, then it is not just the rejection, but everything that was once positive is now negative. You thought you had conquered it, but then something triggers it again, and you have an unusual reaction to rejection because you have RSD. The place you are in is so painful, and there is an inability to express that pain or articulate the feeling. There are those around you who say that you should get over it, that it is just a feeling and you will be okay. But deep down inside you are saying, "No, I can't handle this rejection. I can't run the risk of being rejected again." You play it safe and do everything to avoid feeling the pain. You don't want to go back to that dark place, and you think you have closed the door, but you have actually closed yourself off.

When a shield becomes a prison

It is possible, if you are dealing with extreme reactions to rejection, that seemingly simple things in life can trigger you, causing you to close yourself off to other people, because you try to protect your heart from being rejected again. In fact, everything around you can look great and seem amazing, you smile on your social media accounts and pretend that everything is okay. But on the inside you are living in a prison, tortured by an ongoing stream of negative thoughts and feelings. There are shadows of darkness that fill your mind and heart and it's hard for you to connect with God and the ones you love. You may even push away the ones you love most. You are crying out for help and attention, but because of the walls and the protection you have built around your heart, you push people away. The shield which once protected you from rejection turns out to be a prison. It does not help you at all and is more like a curse. However, because you are so used to it, it becomes a pattern and you are in survival mode. On the inside you wrestle with yourself in silence. What frequently happens is that when you are rejected again, all other moments of rejection resurface and it all mixes together in your mind, forming a toxic cocktail. All of this makes a lot of noise on the inside, drowning out other voices.

> If you don't know how to navigate through rejection, you will end up going in circles

You can end up in a situation in which you no longer try to step out in faith, no longer try to pray through the words and prophecies spoken over your life. You become numb emotionally. You don't walk in the opportunities God gives you because of your fear of rejection. When you grow older and have not learned how to deal with rejection and navigate the valley of despair and hopelessness, you may end up turning your prison into a fortress. This is where you go to hide every time you are triggered by rejection. Facing these extreme feelings of rejection is not about the doors that were open to you, but about dealing with the doors that were closed.

Many leaders experience rejection

As I work with other leaders all around the world, I have learned that this subject is so important to talk about, to give words to feelings that they could not explain. Leaders can experience a lot of rejection, especially by those close to them. Rejection can stop you from walking in faith. It can cause you to become cold, and isolate you. It can dim the light in you, dampen the fire and it will affect the people around you. We have to deal with this, because if you are being used by God on the frontline, you will experience various kinds and levels of rejection and betrayal. If you do not understand the purpose behind rejection, nor know how to navigate through rejection, you will end up going in circles, resulting in exhaustion and discouragement. This will lead to bitterness and eventually giving up.

But, in being rejected, we are in good company! David did not get invited to the party when Samuel came to visit his father, Jesse. And Jesus was rejected on numerous occasions:

- When Joseph and a very pregnant Mary arrived in Bethlehem, there was no room for them in the inn. That's why Mary ended up giving birth to Jesus in a stable surrounded by animals.
- Herod sent soldiers to kill every male child under two years of age in his attempt to kill Jesus.
- When Jesus returned to His hometown of Nazareth, after He read Isaiah 61 and applied the words to Himself, His own townspeople were so enraged they sought to kill Him.
- His own half-brothers did not believe in Him, rejecting His claims of being the Messiah.
- The religious leaders rejected Him as a fraud, a deceiver and a blasphemer, and plotted together how to murder Him.
- One of His disciples, Judas, betrayed Him to the authorities, resulting in His crucifixion. This betrayal is so central to Jesus' life and work that all four Gospels record it and Paul includes it in his reminder to the Corinthian church on the meaning of communion: "The Lord Jesus, on the night he was betrayed, took bread (...)" Every time we take communion we not only remember Jesus' body and blood, but we also remember His betrayal.
- One of Jesus' closest disciples and friends, Peter, denied

knowing Him, and all the disciples abandoned Him in his darkest hour.

- The crowds demanded of Pilate that he crucify Him. When Pilate offered the crowds a choice of freeing Jesus or freeing a notorious criminal named Barabbas, they chose Barabbas and rejected Jesus.
- The soldiers mocked Jesus' claim of being a prophet as they spat on Him and punched Him and rammed a crown of thorns deep into His head.
- Jesus was crucified on a cross—the most shameful and painful death possible. And even as He hung on the cross in agony, even then, rather than the people standing there feeling compassion for His suffering, they mocked Him.
- Then, worst of all, as Jesus hung on the cross, despised and rejected by people (as Isaiah 53:3 prophesied), He was forsaken by God, His Father. God turned His face from Jesus and unleashed on Jesus all His fury for the filth and evil of sin for all the world for all time. Among Jesus' last words were, "My God, my God, why have you forsaken me?" (Matt. 27:46).

From His birth to His death, rejection was a significant theme in Jesus' life. "He came to that which was his own, but his own did not receive him" (John 1:11). "He was despised and rejected by mankind, a man of suffering, and familiar with pain" (Isa. 53:3).

Storms that are directed by God are not nice. But there is a reason for them. He is working on your character, so that you are able to carry the next season that God has for you. Without this storm, your character will not have the strength, the perseverance, the faith and the assurance that it needs. When we look at Joseph and Mary, there were multiple prophecies that needed to be fulfilled regarding the birth of Jesus.

God is working on your character,
so that you are able to carry the next season
that He has for you

It is likely that Joseph and Mary did not realize at the time
how perfectly directed, by God, all of those things were. They
were probably too preoccupied by the rejection at the inn, and
the birth of Jesus. We can now look at this story and see it as
a foundation for our faith in God. We are busy navigating the
storm while He is directing all of the events in the background,
so that everything will be ready for us when we come out on
the other side of the storm.

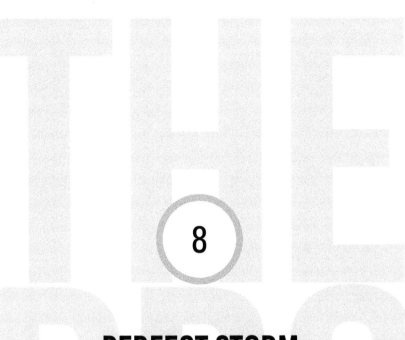

8

PERFECT STORM

When everything happens at once

I wrote this chapter for people who have been called to work on the frontline, in ministries, churches and organizations. The things I talk about in this chapter are partially my own experiences as well as things that I have witnessed up close in the lives of other people around the world. Some things are facts, other things are opinions. Please make sure to read the previous chapters before reading this chapter, in order to understand the context. This chapter was honestly quite challenging to write. I went through a perfect storm myself, and everything in me resisted writing about it. You see, I don't see myself as a victim, nor do I want others to see me as such. My only reason for writing about this is from a desire to serve others and help people who may be going through a similar situation.

A perfect storm

I will first explain why I use the term "perfect storm". In a perfect storm all the elements come together in a chaotic cocktail. If one element is missing, it cannot create a perfect storm. During my time as a maritime officer, I was taught to observe the weather patterns and analyze them. When we saw certain weather patterns, we would know what kind of storm was coming, and whether or not it would be a perfect storm. This would enable us to navigate around the storm, or to prepare ourselves and the ship to go through the storm. A perfect storm does not just appear.

As I just mentioned, there must be several elements that all come together at the same time in a specific way for the perfect storm. Several days before the perfect storm has even formed, you can already see it coming on the weather radar. Before a perfect storm is created, it follows several patterns.

The same thing takes place in the spiritual world, when the devil is setting you up for a perfect storm. The devil follows schematics, an agenda and patterns. He is not creative, he is unable to create and can only copy (and a bad copy at that) and he does the same thing over and over. I can see a clear pattern in the schemes and agenda of satan. They are very clear patterns that create a perfect storm, in an attempt to destroy as much as possible in a very short time.

> A perfect storm often affects your family, friends and the ministry or church connected to you

So by studying the weather patterns, as I did as a maritime officer, we can see that a perfect storm is coming. When we know the patterns, we know which factors we need to keep an eye on. All of us should do that in our lives, because 99.9 percent of people are not aware that a perfect storm is in the making, because it is not their focus. That is why many are ambushed by a perfect storm. When it hits in the natural world, it causes chaos and many people have to leave their homes. Most are unprepared, often not even aware, that a perfect storm could hit them.

A spiritual perfect storm

Years ago, I went through just such a perfect storm, in which the enemy tried to destroy me from every direction at once. It was absolutely horrible. But now God is using this experience to help other people as they go through a perfect storm. When people go through a perfect storm it does not come suddenly. It may feel like it comes suddenly but behind the scenes, evil powers had already secretly partnered with people to fuel this perfect storm. A perfect storm that comes against a person often affects their family, friends and the ministry or church connected to that person. It can be a bitter cocktail of all three storms at once, and you could say it looks like a tornado when you see how overwhelming it can be and how much destruction it can cause. People who live in a tornado area know what to do when a tornado hits. They go to the shelter, or they leave the area that is about to be hit by the storm.

This is one of the things you have to do when a perfect storm hits you. Find a shelter, which can be your home or some other place; find a place where you feel safe and nurtured, where you can be taken care of and where you are surrounded by wise men and women. There is not much you can do the moment a perfect storm hits you. Spiritually speaking, your hiding place is being with the Lord, listening to what He says about you, your now and your future! There is spiritual place called the "table of the Lord" where you can sit with *Him* in the midst of enemies and darkness; a place where Jesus wants to feed you, restore you and encourage you. It is not a place of weakness but of strength.

Remember that there was a time in Jesus' life that He and His family had to hide for a while in a foreign nation, Egypt. Moses had to hide himself for a period of time, David had to hide himself for a while, and the list goes on and on. There are both men and women in the Bible who experienced a perfect storm and had to hide. The Holy Spirit even led them as to where and how to hide. The Holy Spirit will help and lead those people who need to hide and find shelter in Him.

Weathering the storm

A perfect storm feels terrible, ugly, chaotic and destructive. In fact, this is the purpose behind the perfect storm. The purpose of this storm is to cause you to be disoriented. You no longer know who you are, where you are, or where you were headed, and therefore have no clue how you can get out of it. Remember, though, that God always has the last say, and not the storm. He is with you in this storm and the Holy Spirit will help and lead you, down to the very details of what to do and what not to do. It's possible that you don't feel the Holy Spirit, but He is there and will talk to your spirit and give you step-by-step directions. Remember that the Holy Spirit is also called the "Spirit of wisdom and revelation" (Eph. 1:17).

When you get through the storm well, it will speed up every promise on your life and release you into your full purpose and destiny. Not only that, but everything the perfect storm tried to kill and everything it destroyed will be given back to you in double portions. Many times, the perfect storm hits you the very moment you are at the point of breakthrough.

Going through a perfect storm is emotionally very uncomfortable; everything around you is shaken and unstable. People question you and your integrity. You often cannot defend yourself and, in many cases, trust is broken. People who were close to you, or worked close to you, are often used to fuel this perfect storm. And while you are in the middle of this storm, people who are not in the thick of it will doubt you and cease to trust you. They will start to question you, your actions and your motives. Things will be said about you, things you never wanted anyone to say about you. What frequently happens during a perfect storm, things you have said in the past, or in private to people, are exposed and often taken out of context. People who were always a bit jealous of you, but were nice to your face because of, for example, your position as a leader and because they could profit from being in your proximity, are suddenly against you and say things that shock your world. Things you have done wrong in the past, or that, in hindsight, you could have handled better, are now used against you. What often happens is that in your attempts to defend yourself, your words are misunderstood. Words you spoke in the past come back as a boomerang, but they are now taken out of context and twisted. People around you whom you trusted have already

turned away from you in their hearts and communicated this
with others behind your back.

Gossip and juicy details

When you are a public person, often the media is already involved before you are aware of it. It feels like the whole world
knows what the media writes about you in various articles.
Just going to the supermarket, or taking your kids to school,
can feel unsafe, and you feel ashamed and embarrassed. Sometimes friends who are also in ministry suddenly don't want
to be seen with you because of your situation, and hanging
around you could affect their ministry. It may feel like they
care more about their reputation and ministry than they care
about you. They distance themselves from you.

You find out who your true friends are in these moments,
those who have pure motives and hearts. During the perfect
storm you feel like you are losing your reputation, your credi-
bility, favor with people; your heart sinks to the bottom of your
soul. You suffer from stress, panic and chaos. You feel bruised,
betrayed and rejected. You cannot see how it will ever be okay
again; there is no way back from this, of that you are sure. It
is finished. It is hard to trust people, yourself, and sometimes
even God anymore. And in the end, you can partner with the
thought of disqualifying yourself.

Most people have no idea what you are going through.
They don't understand. All of this affects your family and you
are dealing with multiple issues, people and circumstances.
Many times, it affects your friendships, finances, partners
and in some cases you also have to deal with what has been
communicated about you through the media. Often the media
has worked in secret for a while, gathering intel, gossip and
juicy details. They try to find any dirt they can on you, from
the past or present. They are not interested in your side of the
story, or even in facts. They just want a juicy story that will sell

well. They will do whatever it takes to prove a point, whether or not that point is true or valid. They use the power of the media to create a narrative, making it very hard to defend yourself.

Gjakova, Kosovo

In my early years, in 1999, the Lord called me to be a missionary in Kosovo. This was a place where a terrible war had taken place. I did not know at that time, this was an area where there had been many tensions for hundreds of years, and that it was on the dividing line of Christianity and Islam. I had been praying in the "Blackbird's Field", a large field in central Kosovo. It was the site of the Battle of Kosovo in 1389, which took place between the "Christian" Balkan Alliance and the "Muslim" Ottoman armies. This is where Islam was stopped from penetrating Europe. Thousands died there, and there is still a huge spiritual battle raging there.

As a missionary I worked for Derek Prince Ministries and a Dutch foundation, De Brug. My duties were to provide the widows and orphans with spiritual and practical support. It was a war situation and I saw a lot of destruction up close. I also witnessed many miracles and signs and saw people from different religious backgrounds come to Jesus. After having worked as a missionary for a year, a revival broke out in the Gjakova area where I was. Gjakova also means "city of blood", and in that city and the surrounding areas many men had been murdered, and there were large mass graves. The Holy Spirit began to move powerfully, and Jesus broke through the dark atmosphere. There were three places of worship for another religion, and in the middle of them we built a revival center for the many converts. What happened there was really very special. More and more people came to faith and were delivered and healed. We truly experienced a revival in the midst of darkness.

Demonic powers

Early one morning, the atmosphere in the room I was sleeping in changed. It was suddenly freezing cold, and clouds of flies came up out of nowhere as I was waking up. I jumped up out of bed and opened the windows in an attempt to chase the flies away. When I finally laid back down in bed, large rats appeared out of seemingly nowhere, and walked towards me. I was able to chase them away as well. When I wanted to make some coffee, a figure appeared in the room where I was staying. The best I can describe it was that it looked like it had two heads and one body; the heads each looked in a different direction. It was dark and resembled the symbol on the Albanian flag, the same flag used in Kosovo at the time. This dark figure was trying to intimidate me and I suddenly realized I was dealing with a stronghold over that area.

> God always has the last say,
> not the storm

That morning when I left the house and had to pass Russian and Italian war tanks from the Kosovo force to get bread, I saw graffiti on the outside of our house. It said: "We are satan's people, go home." Someone who I knew well and who had not dealt with certain satanic issues from the past, therefore leaving a door open to dark spiritual forces, started to manifest demonic powers. The demonic world started to speak to our team through this person, and their head twisted around nearly a full 360 degrees. This demonic power told us we had to leave the area or something bad would happen to us. Fortunately, we were able to bind this demonic power and send it away. This was my first collision with a dark spiritual power. I also understood then that we must be aware that we are fighting "the good fight" (1 Tim. 6:12) and that we should not occupy territories to which we are not called.

Not much later, various crises broke out in the leadership of the organizations I worked for, and the international organization in Kosovo wanted to close. Also, the employer I worked for was fired and further major crises broke out. It was then that I saw up close that a demonic force is often behind a perfect storm. Remember that after one and a half years living as missionary, taking care of hundreds of broken, traumatized war victims from another religion, we started to see a mighty outpouring of the Holy Spirit and many people started to give their lives to Jesus, and then all hell broke loose.

The spirit behind the storm

In the case of Jesus, God Himself was behind the plan of the cross. But we also see that when Jesus was crucified, all of hell came after Him. How did Jesus respond to His perfect storm? "Father, forgive them, for they do not know what they are doing" (Luke 23:34). Jesus did not blame the people around Him for being used to create this perfect storm. He forgave them. Jesus knew that some people who betrayed Him or denied Him were used by God. No one murdered Jesus, God was behind the plan of the crucifixion so that everyone could be saved and receive eternal life!

It's almost unimaginable how the people around us, who sometimes were our closest confidants, who worked alongside us in God's Kingdom for many years, maybe even family members or others close to us, can hurt us! But we must keep in mind that we are not fighting against people. Remember that "our struggle is not against flesh and blood, but against the rulers, against the authorities, against the powers of this dark world and against the spiritual forces of evil in the heavenly realms" (Eph. 6:12). Your soul will say that it is people, but we have to choose to look with our spiritual eyes, and then we will see that many times a spirit is speaking through other people, and it is not always the Spirit of God. In many cases there is a demonic spirit behind the perfect storm. I don't like to focus on this too much, because in all that I do I want to focus on Jesus, His Word, His promises, His wisdom and His counsel. On the other hand, if you are called to work on the frontline you must be aware of the strategy of the devil. It is not your focus, but you should at least be aware of it. What I'm about to share is an opinion, something I'm personally convinced is very probable. Behind a perfect storm is often a similar dark force, and it has a name: Leviathan.

Leviathan

In the book of Isaiah, Leviathan is a sea serpent symbolizing Israel's enemies. In the book of Job, Leviathan is a fire-breathing crocodile, perhaps the personification of an aspect of creation that is beyond human understanding or control. Leviathan is *Livyatan* in Hebrew; in Jewish mythology, it is a prehistoric sea serpent (Isa. 27:1). St Thomas Aquinas described Leviathan as the demon of envy, first in punishing the corresponding sinners (*Expositio super Iob ad litteram*). In the sixteenth century the German theologian Peter Binsfeld also said Leviathan is the demon of envy, as one of the seven Princes of Hell corresponding to the seven deadly sins. Leviathan is more than a sea monster; he is a principality. He is regarded among the principalities as the mighty.

Leviathan is a predator spirit; when he captures his prey, he doesn't allow them to go easily. In the Greek, he is called "the god of chaos" meaning "the god of confusion". When Leviathan attacks you, he makes you confused, afraid and unable to find a solution to your problems. Leviathan is a dragon; he has a serpentine nature. In Psalm 74:13-14, he is referred to as "the monster in the waters": "It was you who split open the sea by your power; you broke the heads of the monster in the waters. It was you who crushed the heads of Leviathan and gave it as food to the creatures of the desert." The Bible says in Job 41:19-31 that fire comes out from his mouth and nostrils. He is not an ordinary dragon but a snakelike dragon. He was the principality in charge of the multiple attacks on Job. Job got confused and began wondering why he lost everything he had in one day. He didn't know that it was the principality called Leviathan that was in charge of his case.

In Job 41, God revealed the nature of Leviathan to Job. This means it is something we need to deal with because it is a principality that is always confronting humanity. Leviathan was also the power behind Pharaoh (Ezek. 29:1-5). He was responsible for the prosperity and commerce of Egypt. The crown on Pharaoh's head had a design of a serpent on top of it, which symbolized the god (Leviathan) in the sea the Egyptians worshiped. God addressed Pharaoh in Ezekiel 29:1-5 as the great dragon that lies in the river. It simply means behind the Pharaoh was a god called Leviathan, the great dragon that was lying in the river Nile in Egypt. That is why Pharaoh wakes up very early to worship this god in the river (Ex. 8:20). Also, when Moses was born, in order to kill him, an estimated 2,000-3,000 children were sacrificed to this great dragon. Yet, Moses escaped.

The slaying of Leviathan

To deal with this enemy, we must look to the Word. Scripture describes the defeat of a spirit called Leviathan: "In that day, the LORD will punish with his sword—his fierce, great and powerful sword—Leviathan the gliding serpent, Leviathan the coiling serpent; he will slay the monster of the sea" (Isa. 27:1; Ps. 104:24-26). While there are a number of theories about what these verses describe, most scholars have linked Leviathan with the Nile crocodile. But Leviathan is clearly more than a crocodile. Asaph states in Psalm 74:14 that Leviathan has multiple heads, and Isaiah sees him as a spiritual enemy; a supernatural serpent that must be defeated. Serpents and dragons embody the work of Satan throughout Scripture. Leviathan's crooked path can be traced from the serpent in Eden to the dragon of Revelation. Thank God, we've been given authority " to trample on snakes and scorpions and to overcome all the power of the enemy (...)" (Luke 10:19). In the end, Leviathan is slain.

When you get through the storm well, it will release you into your full purpose and destiny

---

Leviathan's clear mission is to destroy the lives of God's people by dividing them in subtle ways. The name "Leviathan" comes from a root word that means "to twist"—one of his primary tactics. Leviathan twists your words, so that the other person listening hears something very different than what you said. Like the crocodile, Leviathan approaches its prey slyly, just under the surface. When the moment is right, it strikes explosively with one aim—taking hold of its victims and twisting them apart. This brings division between people. Separation attacks relationships subtly. A wife wonders, "What did my husband mean by that?", or with the right amount of demonic spin, confusion and suspicion are sown between the best of friends. The enemy twists things just a little bit more each time, and if we don't discern it, things can snap. Even apostles can fall into a spirit of division and go separate ways over unimportant matters (Acts 15:36-40). The tactic is always the same: Twisting and separation, twisting and separation—and you never see it coming.

So although it is not nice to have people believe lies about you, that is what Leviathan does in people. In most cases, if you just give them to the Lord and keep on doing what you are supposed to do for the Lord, you will be blessed and eventually people will know the truth. "If your enemy is hungry, give him food to eat; if he is thirsty, give him water to drink. In doing this, you will heap burning coals on his head, and the LORD will reward you" (Prov. 25:21-22). So keep your peace on, and do what the Holy Spirit directs you to do and let the Lord take care of your adversaries. God is good and will correct those who need correcting and will bless those who are pure, righteous and humble before Him.

So when Leviathan comes raging in with a perfect storm, you often don't know what hit you. You may have felt that something was off in the spirit, but you could not quite put your finger on it. That is why it is important that we recognize the patterns, so that we have a clear warning that an attack is coming.

What do you do in the storm?

But what if you see an attack coming, or you are in the middle of a perfect storm? What do you do? The first thing is that you need to model yourself on Jesus. "Father, forgive them, for they do not know what they are doing" (Luke 23:34). Watch out with social media too! That is *never* the place to judge others, throw mud, or even justify yourself, your actions or your words. In fact, social media can be the devil's playground. So if you want some advice: Stay as far away as you can from using social media to prove you are right, or point out how wrong the other person or group is. Stay far away from the devil's playground and don't play in it, for you will open a door to poisonous interactions and lose favor with the Lord. The Bible says in Romans: "You, therefore, have no excuse, you who pass judgment on someone else, for at whatever point you judge another, you are condemning yourself, because you who pass judgment do the same things. Now we know that God's judgment against those who do such things is based on truth.

So when you, a mere human being, pass judgment on them and yet do the same things, do you think you will escape God's judgment? Or do you show contempt for the riches of his kindness, forbearance and patience, not realizing that God's kindness is intended to lead you to repentance?" (Rom. 2:1-4). You would think Paul is talking about social media here, right?!

The fact is that this perfect storm uses munition that can be found in your past. It is no use denying your past, and if you do, it will backfire. What you do need to do in response to such a storm is this:

- Start by taking responsibility for your own actions and if you have made mistakes, don't hide them.
- Form a group of leaders around you where you share your process, your pain and the things you are going through. Handle the consequences of your actions in a godly manner. Ask for advice from other trusted leaders around you.
- Stay away from interviews, media or social media. Don't fight back through media, social media or articles. If necessary, make a short statement; let other leaders with experience review this statement before you release it.
- Guard your own heart. Having lots of emotions is healthy, but don't let anger take root in your heart, and do not let emotions rule. Experiencing emotions is different from having them control you.
- Get counseling for a while if necessary.
- Read or listen to positive and empowering preaching and teaching, and speakers who have gone through storms and difficult situations.
- Speak the promises of God over your life out loud (I added a list of declarations of God's promises at the end of the book)
- Take time to worship, pray and read the Word.
- Don't fight the devil on his own territory.
- Hide, rest and eat well, and make sure you start exercising. Take time with your family or the people dear to you.
- When the storm is over, start to rebuild in a better way.
- Focus on the Psalms in these seasons of process; every

emotion you can experience during a perfect storm is mentioned in the Psalms, as David went through several perfect storms. For instance, you may cry the prayer David cried:

> Save me, O God, for the waters have come up to my neck. I sink in the miry depths, where there is no foothold. I have come into the deep waters; the floods engulf me. I am worn out calling for help; my throat is parched. My eyes fail, looking for my God. Those who hate me without reason outnumber the hairs of my head; many are my enemies without cause, those who seek to destroy me. I am forced to restore what I did not steal. You, God, know my folly; my guilt is not hidden from you.
> – PSALM 69:1-5

You are not a victim

And, yes, all these emotions and terrible things you are going through are destructive and awful, but you are not a victim. You have to take full responsibility in this season for your words, your thoughts, your attitude and your actions. Don't become a victim of the circumstances. It's very easy to adopt a victim mentality after or during what you are experiencing due to all these almost traumatic emotions and events that no human should have to go through. If you don't understand the purpose behind this, then yes, it's very easy to partner with that thought, but it will not help you move forward. When you partner with victim mentality there's a possibility that you will become bitter and lose your faith, and even worse, you may end up letting go of the calling of God on your life.

The fact is you can walk through the storm in faith, with the right attitude and character! This is what people see. People look at how you respond to the storm. People will forget what has been said in the media within several months. There is news every day. It feels like a crazy rollercoaster if you are in the middle of it, but the media will not write about you for months; most of the time the story will be featured in several media outlets for several days. Everyone, including all kinds of Christian leaders and ministries, will have an opinion about you and will gladly publish it. Don't be afraid of that; most Christians who throw mud at you in response to the stories in the media were never your friends to begin with and probably never will be, and the judgment they put on you will come back to them like a boomerang. Jesus was very clear about judging other people. We just read Romans 2:1-4 about that.

My dear friend, know that the storm you are going through will pass, and that your responsibility in this storm is to hold on to your connection with God. Don't trust your emotions or feelings, don't rely on people around you who are not full of faith, don't blame God, but stand on God's Word, keep pressing into His presence, and you will see over time that God is able to restore and bless you with a double portion of what the enemy tried to steal.

Again, people will watch how you walk through this perfect storm. There is a purpose behind the rejection, the pain, behind being bruised and betrayed. That which satan thought would destroy you will in fact be used by God to advance the Kingdom of God and pierce the works of darkness. And this will also be seen by the people around you.

In Daniel 3, we read that Shadrach, Meshach and Abednego were thrown into the furnace, yet they came out of the fire with not even hair that was singed nor did they smell like smoke, because God supernaturally protected them. These three young men placed all of their trust in God. If you are in the fire, trust Him that He is with you in the fire and that after this season of fire and smoke you will not be burned or even smell like fire. In the end, this will be part of your testimony.

HOW TO KEEP ON GOING

Navigating the worst storms

In the previous chapters I have shared several things on the transformation that takes place during a process. We have looked at why storms happen, what causes them and what lessons can be learned during these storms. I have tried to share some of the knowledge I have gained from my own experiences, and the storm I have overcome. So how do you keep on going when a storm comes crashing into your life? What do you hold on to when everything is shaking? I hope that by telling a bit of my story, I will be able to assist you so that you too can keep on going when the process in your life seems overwhelming.

There was a season in my life in which I went through a perfect storm. Things that I could have handled better, processes that God wanted to lead me through and demonic attacks all took place at once. Before it all started, I was a married man with a worldwide ministry and I was senior pastor of a church. Sometime later on I was suddenly a single father taking care of our three young kids full-time, and felt the most alone I have ever felt in my entire life. This was the season in which I became convinced that God could no longer use me, that I had disqualified myself and that everything was over. There was no coming back from this, or so I thought.

Thick fog

A few years ago, I had an interesting experience after a New Year's Eve celebration. I was driving from Harderwijk where the family party had been, a place in the Netherlands where I lived for a while, to Ermelo, where we lived at the time. It is a short drive of around ten minutes. I had driven that route probably thousands of times—I can see it clearly in my mind's eye and know every turn, every bit of this road. But that night there was a very thick fog. There is often fog in the Netherlands, but nothing like this. The fog that night was so thick that eventually one of us had to get out of the car and walk ahead to see where to go, because the road was no longer visible. We were just a few hundred yards away from home, it was literally right around the corner, but we could not see it. As one led the way walking, the other drove slowly so we could get home. There was no other way to move forward because of how thick the fog was.

Learn to trust God's Spirit to lead you through the thick fog

---

The perfect storm felt like that—as if I had ended up in such a thick fog that I could no longer see anything, even though I was on familiar ground. I felt as though I should be able to see where I was, but could not because of the blinding fog. No matter where I turned, no matter where I looked, I could not see. Not to the left, nor to the right. There was nothing ahead of me and nothing behind me. And just like when you turn your car lights on brightly in a thick fog, it actually blinds you even more and you see less. That only made things worse. That is what it felt like, like a fog had descended on all areas of my life, no matter where I looked. I could no longer think straight. I had no idea how I was going to get through the next day. I felt alone and was unsure of where to turn.

When God draws near

In the evenings, when I had put the children to bed and I sat by myself on the sofa, I would feel God draw near to me. I would make a point to turn on worship music and as I sat there, the tears would flow. The pain, rejection and fear, really all of the emotions that David describes in the Psalms, would come to the surface, all mixed together. When there was no one else around, when I did not have to put on a brave face, when it was just me and God, everything would come out. And I would sense His presence. Looking back, those were very valuable moments. There was a depth to those experiences, things that happened deep down in my soul and spirit, that eventually made me a stronger person.

I became convinced that when it seems like you will lose everything, or when you have lost everything, when people question and doubt you, when you are unable to share the whole story, God does not question or doubt you. He knows the truth. He knows all the details of what happened, why it happened and how you feel. I have always clung to certain verses in the Bible. One that is special to me is this Psalm:

> The Lord is my shepherd, I lack nothing. He makes me lie down in green pastures, he leads me beside quiet waters, he refreshes my soul. He guides me along the right paths for his name's sake. Even though I walk through the darkest valley, I will fear no evil, for you are with me; your rod and your staff, they comfort me. You prepare a table before me in the presence of my enemies. You anoint my head with oil; my cup overflows. Surely your goodness and love will follow me all the days of my life, and I will dwell in the house of the LORD forever.
> – PSALM 23

The knowledge that He would prepare a table for me "in the presence of my enemies", that He would anoint my head with oil, was very comforting, though I did not feel like those were happening at the time. I experienced what it was like to know that there was favor on my life, but not feel it—when everything seems dark around you, yet somehow life goes on and you have to keep functioning when you feel like your own life is falling apart.

Oh, poor me…

I know that God saved me during this storm, that He kept me afloat. But I also made a choice to not give up. I was not going to give in. I was going to keep on going, even if that meant I could only move forward by walking slowly, carefully feeling my way in the fog, and was unable to run for a while. I never stayed in my bed with a duvet covering my head, wallowing in self-pity and a victim mentality. I sure felt like it, though. I wanted to. But I didn't. Of course it was tempting to think, "Oh, poor me …" I communicated my feelings to those closest to me, those I could trust. But I never gave up. My soul told me that I would never be happy, that nothing good would ever happen to me again, but my spirit knew otherwise and always came out on top.

I think that is what we would call the spirit of faith, as it is not dependent on our emotions, which stem from our soul, nor dependent on our body—because the Spirit of God partners with our spirit, and God's Spirit works through us. I needed to learn to not always listen to my feelings. Yes, my feelings were and are valid. I am allowed to be sad, to be frustrated, even angry, but in the end, it is the Spirit and the Word of God who determine the direction to take in the thickest fog. Our emotions, feelings or our situation should not determine where to go. That is something I learned in those dark moments, as I stumbled forward, learning as I went to trust God's Spirit to lead me through the thick fog. I knew that even though I felt terrible, even though I could not see how any good could come of this situation, I had to get through the day, I had to be there for my children. I focused on them and let the world pass me by, regardless of what people said or thought about me. God is my source, my joy, and I need to find all that I needed in Him.

When life is not how you imagined it

It may seem easy to say that I needed to learn that all I needed I would find in God. But getting there was hard. It was one of the hardest lessons I have ever had to learn. I could not find satisfaction or fulfillment from being on stage, because that was not an option then. I could not find recognition or any satisfaction from being on social media, as that was a hornets' nest. I could only find my fulfillment and satisfaction in God. It was God and Mattheus, Mattheus and God, and my three children. That was an interesting process, in which I was on a rollercoaster and I experienced things that I never thought would happen. My life did not look like how I had imagined it, not even anything close to it.

How did I get there? I was married and we shared three beautiful, amazing children. Then life took a turn in a very different direction, and suddenly I found myself alone, a single father of three, and wondering what had hit me. My whole life turned upside down and the ideas, thoughts, dreams and expectations for my life, and the future, were gone in an instant. This period, in which I unwillingly went through a divorce, in which I found myself trying to juggle being a single father, the care of my children, dealing with my own emotions, and the wildest stories being told about me in the press, was probably one of the hardest things I have ever experienced. The craziest things happened and were said, but I had to keep on going. I was confronted with many new situations in my life, and I had no answers for them. I would go to God with these things, and He would speak to me in detail about what I should do, what I shouldn't do, what I should say and when to stay silent. He who has the wisdom of the ages gave me the wisdom I needed to navigate this storm, where to place my feet and how to move forward, be it ever so slow. God truly led me through all of these processes.

People and things sent by God

God would send people my way, often total strangers, who would help me for a period of time to get through a certain part of my storm. Sometimes I would meet someone who, just like I, had gone through a divorce though they did not want to, and who walked by my side for a while. Or when I was given a book about divorce by a Christian author that I had not heard of previously. This book gave me all kinds of tips and keys on what to do. And then there was another book by a Baptist pastor about divorce and remarriage and what the Bible has to say about those subjects. It was very helpful, because that was something that I was really thinking about in regards to being a (unwilling) divorcee—what does God's Word say about all of this?

The things that really helped me in this season were God's Word, worshiping Him, and the small group of friends who still believed in me. They kept telling me I was going to pull through, that I would make it. Also, where would I be without my Christian psychologist? I had many meetings with him, and to this day I am so grateful for all his assistance. He was so very helpful. I would go there every Monday, for two years. Every week I would be back there, sitting in his office, even though I often didn't want to go. Initially all the meeting consisted of was me sitting there, crying my eyes out, going through boxes of tissues at a time. Eventually, though, the meetings turned into conversations, contemplating various things and talking about subjects that really helped me get through that process.

I truly experienced that God sent just the right people, at the right time. I had to trust Him in that. My job was to not give up. To keep on walking, stumbling forward. To not do anything if God had not told me to do it. I really had trust Him in my process, because I knew that I did not know anything. I had difficulties believing the promises of God upon my life: "But You, God, are the one who has the final say.

I cannot do this, so You will have to. You will need to make a way through the jungle." At the time I had no idea what was around the corner, or who—Laura, my beautiful wife, given to me by God, who brought so much healing to my life. But there were a lot of things I had to work through before that, many layers that needed to be peeled back. And I had to wait for God, and keep moving forward.

Self-care

A vital part of getting through the storm is self-care. It may sound selfish, but actually, when you are in a very stressful situation, it is so important to take care of yourself. That means eating well, exercising and getting enough fresh air. I made a conscious choice to exercise; I went for walks and cycled. I don't like walking, but I did it anyway, as well as swimming. I stayed active and made sure I met people, connected with people. I took the time to talk with people, that was important too.

> He who has the wisdom of the ages gives you
> the wisdom to navigate this storm

I talked a lot, especially with my best friends, my parents, and of course I also had professional counseling. I even had a season in which I received some medication during the worst crisis period to help me sleep. This was temporary and supervised by professionals, but it helped me get the much-needed sleep in order to keep on going. It is so important to get sleep during a stressful period and, if needed, medication can help, I believe as long as it is not too long and under professional supervision.

Besides all this, the board of the church I was leading and I decided that I would take a temporary break. I needed to pause as I was in the depth of my crisis, not keep on rushing forward, blindly, but focus on my own healing and be there for my children. That takes time, and I was given that time and the opportunity to take a break to get back on my feet. You see, wounded leaders that just keep on going, without working on their healing and the much-needed self-care and restoration, are leaders who will wound others. This timeout period lasted three months, after which I slowly eased back into the work and ministry surrounded by a wonderful group of family, friends, national and international leaders.

Being accountable

Accountability is very important too. I was accountable to my board and to some well-known international and national leaders, especially during the turmoil of that time. It is easy to be offended, to want to defend yourself, especially when you feel like a lot of injustice has been done. I felt like I was being treated unjustly, that there were things said that were not justified, but I chose to submit myself to the board. These people were not afraid to say what they thought, and they were wise and knowledgeable. They had walked alongside me for many years and when they gave me advice, I listened and implemented it. To be honest, I cannot remember them saying anything, advising anything, especially that year, that I said I wouldn't do, or that I would do differently. When you are in a storm, when you are going through a process, you are very vulnerable, so I am extremely grateful to the board, who stood by me and advised me during that time. I was transparent with them, and I showed them what I was going through in that process. I think that anyone who goes through a crisis, goes through a process, needs to share this with someone. Anyone who has been unjustly accused of things needs someone they can trust and talk to about what is happening in their hearts. Let people in, let them read the words written by you or others, let them see, let them think with you. I did that at the time, and this truly helped me in later processes.

Act like royalty

Take the high road. Act like the royalty you are. Don't throw mud, don't slander others. Don't drop down to their level. Make sure that you do not broadcast everything that is said and done. God will vindicate you, and He will make sure injustice is dealt with. Acting like royalty also means taking responsibility for the things I have done, for my own life, no matter how painful that may be, and for the things that I could have and should have done differently. I never hurt anyone on purpose, but there were certain situations that I could have handled better, or in which I should have responded differently. Being royalty, as children of God, we have to hold ourselves to a higher standard and that means taking the high road; it means taking responsibility.

Taking responsibility is not just for the things of the past that can no longer be changed, but also for your life right now, and what you do with it. When I started to take real responsibility for myself, for the past, it gave me a sense of control. I felt like I had a little more grip on my life and it wasn't just things happening to me. Instead of blaming everyone and everything for the storm, I took responsibility, and with that I was no longer allowing my circumstances to control me.

The time came when there was more peace in my life, and that I was able to enjoy the little things more. I learned to live in the here and now, and from my heart. People have said to me that Mattheus before the crisis and Mattheus after the crisis are very different people. Before the crisis I was less approachable, perhaps also less authentic. When you go through a crisis you learn to communicate from your heart, live from a place of being genuine. Someone said to me, "Hey, Mattheus, this crisis has made you a more beautiful person, it has brought you closer to God." That is how it feels.

It has not been easy. It is really difficult. I do really identify with Shadrach, Meshach and Abednego, who were thrown into the fiery furnace—we read about this in Daniel 3. I used to think to myself that I did not want to go through the fire, because it is no fun. I thought perhaps it might purify me, and it did. You see, when those guys came walking out of the furnace, they did not even smell of smoke. I could not imagine that until I was in the fire myself. And now that I have come out, I can testify that it is true. God really is there in the furnace with you, and when you go through the process with Him, you will come out without smelling of smoke. In fact, you step into the fulfillment of God's promises over your life and your true calling and destiny.

Favor after the storm

When you have gone through the storm, there is supernatural fruit, extraordinary favor and divine blessing, because you got through it and God has seen that you are to be trusted. Now, I am not saying you need to go through a storm in order to have the favor of God in your life, as we are all blessed by God. However, we all go through periods where feelings, emotions and unpleasant circumstances do not influence the favor on our lives. We think it does, and then when things go well, we think we are favored. That is a truth I have learned—what our life looks like does not determine whether or not we are favored.

Circumstances can be awful, you can feel horrible, and yet the favor of God is still on your life because it does not depend on your circumstances or how you feel. I have learned to live more by faith and from my spirit, instead of looking at my circumstances and thinking to myself, "I don't feel happy, so the favor of God must not be on my life." That is truly a lie. And when you think something like that, you start to live from a performance mindset, trying to do things in order to be favored. But God did not tell you to do those things.

But what if you have given up?

I want to share something more that really helped me while I was in the storm and when I was tempted to give up. I embraced the mystery of not understanding why things were happening in my life. I got to the point of not knowing, not understanding, and I kept going in circles. My head hurt from thinking, considering things over and over and over. But then there was a moment in which I was able to let go of all the questions, and that I did not need to know "why". It may sound like a cliché—not knowing why, but only knowing that God is good. This is the position: "You are God and though I don't understand, I trust You," even if you are angry, sad, when you don't understand.

If you are at the point of giving up, or have given up, I want to tell you that it is not bad to be in a season of not knowing. It is not wrong to say, "I just don't know anymore. I don't have an answer and I am just going to leave all these questions here for now, unanswered. I am going to put the calling of God, the promises spoken over me, right here and just let it sit for a while." If you are reading this book, then you haven't really given up. You are just on pause for a moment. Those who really do give up are often those who have had identity crises their entire lives to a greater or lesser degree, and who have never fully surrendered themselves to God and His guidance. They seem okay at the top of the mountain, but down in the valley is where you see what they are truly made of. Their faith is like the house built on the sand, the wind and waves of the storm come and all is washed away; nothing is left standing (Matt. 7:26-27). The storm exposes the kind of foundation a life is built upon.

There are those whose lives truly are built on a firm foundation, on the Rock, Jesus Christ, and when the storms hit, they do not give up. Yes, the wind and the rain may rip off the shutters of their windows, their roof may lose a few shingles, but the house of their life remains standing. They do not give up because their spirit of faith is much stronger than the emotions of their soul.

Unless they work on their healing, wounded leaders will wound others

---

Our soul and flesh must submit itself to our spirit and the Spirit of God. We can only do that if we feed our soul and flesh less, and feed our spirit more. What we put in will come out eventually. We must focus on what we "eat", what we feed our spirit, soul and body on. We are naturally inclined to feed our bodies first, our souls next, and then our spirit may get the leftovers once a week. We cannot live on one meal a week, so why do we expect our spirit to? We must feed our spirit with the things of God, with His Word, with godly input. We need to do this before the storm, but also when we are in the middle of it. We need to feast on God's words of life, we need to speak out life over ourselves, our families, our situations. We need to state what He says about us. We cannot say out loud, "I give up!" because what are we feeding when we do that? Yes, you may feel like giving up. You may feel like you cannot go on. It is okay to acknowledge that you need to rest and replenish your body and soul. We are triune beings, so we must care for all three aspects of our life.

Keep on going

When we go through crises, it is a training ground for our spirits. We learn to speak life, to live in faith, and we grow in our relationship with our God and King. As children of the Most High God, we must learn how to rule and reign. And God can use the crises to teach us how to rule and reign in life—speaking hope into a seemingly hopeless situation; speaking the promises of God over our lives, that which we do not see yet, as if they were.

Imagine if Abraham, Joseph, David, Job, Daniel or Mary, and every single person mentioned in the Bible, had given up in their distress and storms and stopped trusting in God. It was the spirit of faith deep inside of them that kept them believing, hoping and walking. Most of them did not see with their natural eyes what was on the other side of the process; they did not see the other side in the midst of the storm. But because they did not give up, they all experienced mighty miracles, they all became very close to God. Some of them are mentioned in the Bible as a close friend to God (Moses: Ex. 33:11) or a man after God's heart (David: 1 Sam. 13:14). Through the process we see them being deeply rooted as friend and son of God and we see God's extreme favor, blessings and breakthrough on their life after they walked with Him through the process.

The same applies to you in this process you are going through. It's you and Father God, who is your best friend in all of this, and you will walk with Him through the process and walk with Him out of the process, experiencing an acceleration and speed in God's purpose and calling upon your life. The process is used as a springboard to launch you into exactly the place God wants you to be. So do not allow the feelings that arise during a storm to take control. Once you see what God is doing through the storm, once you see how valuable the lessons learned are, you will be able to rule and reign in all areas of life.

So hang in there. There is a reason for all of this, and a purpose for the storm. You are being made into the man or woman of God that He intended you to be, so that you can be more than victorious.

Your breakthrough is around the corner. I did not know what was on the other side of the door. But I kept trusting and leaning on the Lord. I know now what is on the other side of the door and it is amazing, beyond beautiful and powerful. God restored my heart, gave me a beautiful Godly wife and opened doors only He can open. Life is so good and beautiful and we are celebrating the goodness of God daily in our lives.

Dear friend, keep on walking, keep on trusting, don't try to figure everything out. There is light at the end of the tunnel; the supernatural power of God is working for you on your behalf. There's not a single situation that is getting out of hand or that can separate you from the love of Jesus Christ.

> Who shall separate us from the love of Christ? Shall trouble or hardship or persecution or famine or nakedness or danger or sword? As it is written: "For your sake we face death all day long; we are considered as sheep to be slaughtered." No, in all these things we are more than conquerors through him who loved us. For I am convinced that neither death nor life, neither angels nor demons, neither the present nor the future, nor any powers, neither height nor depth, nor anything else in all creation, will be able to separate us from the love of God that is in Christ Jesus our Lord.
> – ROMANS 8:35-39

FULFILLMENT OF
THE PROMISE

Recognizing the seasons

There may be very long and elaborate seasons in which you go through a process, but our growth as Christians looks more like the cycle of seasons than a one-time uphill battle in the storm of a process. I guess you could see it more as an upward cycle, as there are reoccurring seasons. When you read the Bible, and look closely at the stories of our heroes of faith, you can see four different stages or seasons in the cycles. These men and women of God went through these seasons and this usually started after they received a word from the Lord over their life, or were clearly called to perform a certain task. These same seasons are visible in the lives of great men and women of faith in our more recent history, who have since gone to be with the Lord. And there are those alive today whose lives reveal reoccurring seasons, including my own.

The seasons we go through spiritually speaking, are comparable to the seasons we see in our weather; winter, spring, summer and autumn. These seasons are intertwined, yet distinct from each other. One season leads to the next, and they are co-dependent on each other. If there was no winter, there would be no hopeful spring. Without spring we would not know the joy of summer. Without summer, there would not be the rough and tumble of autumn storms. And no autumn storms means no quiet, cool winter, in which things are prepared in secret for spring. Winter may seem dead, especially in countries where the winters are cold. But in the unseen, an amazing process is taking place that will lead to new leaves, growth and an explosion of life.

Seasons in our life

The same thing happens in our lives. It is not always spring or summer. There will be seasons where we lose our leaves, and we may feel exposed and bare. But these leaves are removed in order to make room for new, fresh leaves, and the old leaves of the previous season will not help once spring comes. In the winter things seem to stand still. There is no progress, no movement, or so it would seem. It can even be a bit depressing. There is nothing spectacular, and certainly no fruit. However, there is a process taking place deep down on the inside, invisible to others and sometimes even to ourselves. This process is preparing us for new life, for the new season.

Once spring arrives, it becomes clear what has been happening in secret during the winter season. Suddenly the sun feels warmer, the skies seem brighter and new life and opportunities are released. In the summer season in our lives, we are enjoying the fruit, the luscious green pastures and the flowers. So our lives can be viewed through the lens of cycles. Just as there are four seasons every year, in the same way there are four seasons in the cycle of our processes. Like a tree, we become stronger during the seasons, our roots go deeper in the soil so that like older trees, we can survive any kind of storm. Spiritually we will look more like Jesus as we go through the seasons of life.

What happens in these seasons?

As stated in earlier chapters of this book, processes often start with a prophetic word or a promise spoken over us. Then the prophetic word or promise is tested and we experience distress and pressure. Through this distress and pressure, we enter the third season in the cycle—the development of our character. In other words, our character is being formed in order to carry the weight of the prophetic word over our life. In the fourth season, we enjoy the manifestation of the prophetic word, and we receive new words for the future.

The different seasons in your process cycle:

1. You receive a prophetic word or promise over your life. This is a declaration of God's intentions and plans for your life. A prophetic message from God speaking about your destiny, your future, who you are going to be.

> For I know the plans I have for you," declares the LORD, "plans to prosper you and not to harm you, plans to give you hope and a future.
> – JEREMIAH 29:11

2. The prophetic word is being tested and there is distress. These words of God lead you into a season that challenges you, in which God is working in your heart to remove all of the things that do not belong there. It can seem as though all of the things that provided security before are now shaken and removed. This is a rough and tumble season, a season of strong winds. This can be painful too, but these things are necessary for the next season.

3. The development of your character. Everything that is in your life that prevents the anointing from flowing, every obstacle and every hindrance, needs to be dealt with. This plunges you into a season of distress in which God is working to develop your character. Distress and development often go hand in hand. Sometimes we get so hung up in our distress that we do not allow God to develop us. The development is needed, though, so that we can reach our calling. Once you have gone through this, you will look back and see that even the trauma caused by all of this will be part of your testimony. When there has been enough development, the final part of the process is reached, namely demonstration.

4. The manifestation of the prophetic word. This is the demonstration of everything that God has said over your life before all of this started, and the manifestation of the changes that the process has brought about in you and your character. This is the joyous celebration of you starting to inherit your destiny.

Joseph

If there was ever a man in the Bible who understood process, and who clearly went through all four stages, it is Joseph. His story can be read starting in Genesis 37. Joseph became a true man of God because he came to a place of understanding how God works and how God thinks. Joseph understood process. He submitted to that process and as a result he was personally transformed, so that he could be used by God and be effective for Him, regardless of the situation or circumstances that he encountered. You see, if you are going to be effective for God, and do anything of significance for Him, then you must submit your life to Him and the process. Every time you go through the cycle of the four seasons in the process, your level of intimacy with God will deepen, and your relationship with Him will grow.

> Like a tree, we become stronger during
> the seasons, our roots going deeper

Let's look at the life of Joseph. "Joseph had a dream, and when he told it to his brothers, they hated him all the more" (Gen. 37:5). Joseph shared this amazing promise, this prophetic dream with his brothers. But they despised him for it. They were supposed to be close to him, but they hated him. There is a lot of jealousy in ministry in the body of Christ too. Our brothers and sisters in Christ can be jealous of a promise or prophecy given to another person. Then Joseph shared the dream: "We were binding sheaves of grain out in the field when suddenly my sheaf rose and stood upright, while your sheaves gathered around mine and bowed down to it" (verse 7). His brothers immediately understood the meaning of the dream. How dare he?! He was their little brother, who did he think he was?! "Do you intend to reign over us? Will you actually rule us?" And they hated him all the more because of his dream and what he had said" (verse 8). But Joseph knew this was a promise from God for him, in which his destiny was revealed.

What made his brothers even angrier was when Joseph had a second dream, and shared this with his brothers and his parents. "'Listen,' he said, 'I had another dream, and this time the sun and moon and eleven stars were bowing down to me'" (verse 9). Initially Jacob, his father, was angry, but he decided to keep the dreams in mind. Joseph had two dreams that clearly declared God's plan for his life, and not just his, but for his entire family as well. Both of these dreams pointed to a future in which Joseph would *rule and reign*. Two of the same dreams. Later, when Joseph was to interpret the dreams of Pharaoh, he would state the following: "The reason the dream was given to Pharaoh in two forms is that the matter has been firmly decided by God, and God will do it soon" (Gen. 41:32).

Testing

After Joseph received these two dreams, he would be put into a situation that would prepare him to rule and reign. It's interesting that when somebody receives a prophetic word about leadership, ruling and reigning, they immediately think that this involves a steady upward progression. Yet Jesus stated that "Anyone who wants to be first must be the very last, and the servant of all" (Mark 9:35). We seem to always forget this part. We always think, "Ah, yes, me a leader! Let's go!" The word of God revealed Joseph's destiny and calling. But Joseph was a teenager who was unable to keep his mouth shut in front of his brothers. And after their "warm" response to his first dream, he still didn't get the hint and shared his second dream with his brothers and father. Joseph's brothers hated him, and he needed training, development and maturity to become the man of God he was supposed to be. God had to mold his life to fit his calling.

David's perspective on Joseph is written in Psalm 105, where he said in verses 18 and 19 that until Joseph was ready, until "the word of the LORD had proved him true" (faithful), he was placed in irons and shackles. How many people realize that a prophetic word will test you? This is a reoccurring pattern throughout the entire Bible. And the reality is that every time God speaks to you about something great that is going to take place, He is going to test you on it. The good news is you cannot fail the test. He will let you take it over and over again until you pass it. Even if everyone else writes you off and places a stamp on your forehead "failure", God will not give up on you and He will give you another chance.

Joseph was given a word about him ruling and reigning. Though Isaiah was yet to be born, the verses in Isaiah 60 are applicable to how he must have felt. "Arise, shine, for your light has come, and the glory of the LORD rises upon you (...) Nations will come to your light, and kings to the brightness of your dawn" (Isa. 60:1, 3). He knew that his brothers would bow down before him, and the next thing that happened was that he found himself in a hole in the ground, looking up at them. His life went in the opposite direction of the word he had received. He went from a word on ruling and reigning to becoming the lowest form of humanity. From his position as Daddy's favorite son, pampered and spoiled, he became a slave with no rights and only a life of servitude in his future. It would be the testing that would make Joseph the man that he eventually became. You have to understand that the testing in your life will make you *great*. As you respond to the testing in your life, as you start to understand that it is God allowing the testing to take place, and that it is designed to establish all of the things inside you that God wants to give you, you must know that He will not give these things to you on your terms. That is because He is God and you are *not!*

Joseph is now in the cycle of transformation. He is being dragged along by a current over which he has no power, and he has to go with the flow of change—although the flow is more like a raging river full of debris than a babbling brook. All of this will change him to such an extent that God can use him. There is a divine contradiction that takes place. When you receive a prophetic word, you cannot just move from where you are at the time to the place where you will be when the word is fulfilled. It is a journey, and God will walk with you, though you first must descend into the pit, perhaps even be sold into "slavery", and take a detour through the prison, before you get to the palace. You will not be alone, though. He is there with you.

It is about being, not doing

The whole reason you are being tested, and the reason why it seems that your life is heading in the opposite direction of what was promised and prophesied, is because God wants to take you on a journey. He wants to take you from ministry, the "doing", and He wants to bring you into fellowship with Him, the "being". God can take you into a place where no one wants to know you, nobody wants to be with you, a place where people abandon you, because it is about you and the Lord building a relationship that will stay and last for a lifetime. You receive a word about your life or ministry, and the next thing that happens is that God may move you as far away as you can possibly get from that word or promise. He wants you in a place where you are totally dependent on Him, where you cannot fall back on others, where it is just you and Him. You have to learn to be okay with it being just Him and you.

Even when everyone else has left, He will not. And you have to be there in that place that you know you are in Him and He is in you before you reach that position of leadership, that position in ministry, because that is your foundation. You will have His approval and His love, and that will be all that matters to you.

When He means more to you than anything else in this world, when you can truly say to God, "My soul yearns for you in the night; in the morning my spirit longs for you" (Isa. 26:9), then you are in the right place. When He is the only One that truly matters, the criticism and praise of others will not faze you. There are lessons that you will learn in that alone place with God that you will never forget, and your relationship with Him will sustain you for the rest of your life. So though it seems contradictory, though you are in the opposite place than the promise, it is a journey from revelation to manifestation, a journey from prophecy received to prophecy fulfilled, and on the way you will find that God is the most trustworthy travel partner you could ever want! You will learn to be with God. If you don't know what God is doing, you will feel lost and alone. Once you know what He is doing, the journey may still be awful, but you will not be alone and you will know that you will not just survive but that God is able to use that situation as a platform for breakthrough into your calling, purpose and destiny.

Joseph knew betrayal

Joseph was thrown into a pit. Try to imagine what was said and done when this happened. Joseph went out to meet his brothers, and probably innocently thought he could kind of hang out with them, sitting around the campfire and cracking jokes as they watched the animals. Instead, they grabbed him as soon as he got there and threw him into a pit. They left him there for hours. Initially he probably was shocked when they ripped off his beautiful coat and threw him in there. Then his shock wears off and now he is mad. "Just wait until I tell Dad! You guys will be in trouble for a month!" But nothing happens and they don't respond to him. He gives up shouting at them and sits down on the bottom of the pit. He is cold, tired and hungry. "Okay, guys, you have had your fun! Enough is enough! Get me out of here!" And still they leave him there.

> You cannot fail the test. He will simply let you take it over and over again until you pass it

He goes to sleep, and when he wakes up he sees a bunch of unfamiliar faces peering into the pit. His brothers pull him up and his relief that he is finally out turns to fear when the strangers grab him, chain him and lead him away. By the time he realizes what is happening, they are already riding away and he is yanked by the chains and has to keep up or be dragged behind the camels. He yells to his brothers, "Please stop them! Don't let them take me! Please! This isn't funny anymore! I want to go home! Please! *please!!*" His brothers ignore him and as he is pulled by the chains and they move further away, he realizes that it is not a joke. That it is all very real and he is being taken away from home, away from his brothers, his dad, everything he ever knew. He feels deeply betrayed by those he should have been able to trust the most.

In the Kingdom of God, you are in good company if you have been betrayed. Growing into a position requires that things change. You will be wounded in ministry. You will experience betrayal. All these things are not strange to Jesus.

I want to know Christ—yes, to know the power of his resurrection and participation in his sufferings, becoming like him in his death, and so, somehow, attaining to the resurrection from the dead.
– PHILIPPIANS 3:10-11

Do you really want to participate in his sufferings? You could almost say that you will not grow in the Kingdom unless you are wounded, betrayed and suffer with Christ. Being wounded in the house of our friends, by the people we thought we could trust; feeling the kiss of betrayal on our cheek ... Jesus experienced it all. We feel the pain when our friends walk away from us, when the rooster crows. It is important that we experience betrayal and being wounded spiritually. If we want to experience the fullness of God, if we want to know the power of His resurrection, then we will need to fellowship in his suffering. And once you realize that experiencing these things is part of our growth and our development, it will become easier to forgive those who have hurt you.

Joseph was sold as a slave, and he had to learn how to deal with the betrayal and rejection of his brothers. The word of the Lord will always be tested, often by betrayal and "enslavement". How will you deal with these things? Did Joseph feel all this? Of course he did! The chains that his body was shackled in could be felt down into his very soul. The betrayal was a physical pain. Later, when Joseph imprisoned his brothers for three days to test them, they said, "Surely we are being punished because of our brother. We saw how distressed he was when he pleaded with us for his life, but we would not listen; that's why this distress has come on us" (Gen. 42:21). They did realize what they were doing when they sold him, when he cried out to them to spare his life. But God used their betrayal and Joseph's enslavement to release the ruler in Joseph, and he went through these trials to give birth to his anointing, that would not only save a nation but all of the known world at the time.

God did this

What is interesting is that after Joseph had been through all of the trials and suffering, after having been sold as a slave, he ended up in Potiphar's house. Potiphar was a powerful and influential man. Joseph did well there, and everything he did prospered. Potiphar recognized the favor on Joseph, so much so that Joseph had incredible responsibility. But then again Joseph was betrayed and he was thrown in prison on false charges. After all, who would believe a slave, and a foreign one at that? Joseph must have wondered if he had not yet suffered enough. And how was God's promise, given to him through a dream, ever going to be fulfilled?

After a long period in prison, Joseph is finally released and pardoned, and becomes Pharaoh's right-hand man. His brothers come to Egypt, and when he sees them, there is no anger in his heart, no thought of revenge. His heart is soft and tender, and he sees their remorse for what they did to him. He is concerned about their distress and them being angry with themselves, and then he says, "because it was to save lives that God sent me ahead of you" (Gen. 45:5). Three times Joseph stressed to his brothers that it was not what they had done, but what God had done! God had sent him to Egypt! "Don't worry, it wasn't you, it was God."

Beloved, you need to know that everything done to you by other people can be used by God, and He can save lives through you and the suffering you have been through. Why does God do this? Because it is his way of bringing us to a place of humility, where He deals with all of the things that should not be there. This is the place God brought you to prepare you for the ministry He has planned for you, to save lives!

Incomplete processes

Three times Joseph told his brothers that God had used their actions for good. The truth is that God, in His wisdom and power, allowed these things to take place. He allows these things to push us to a place where we learn humility, servanthood, grace, mercy and kindness. Joseph knew that his brothers were instruments used by God to change him. No, it does not excuse their terrible sin committed against him, but Joseph was able to see God's hand in all of that and was able to view his brothers through a lens of compassion and forgiveness.

Don't make your healing conditional on your vindication

If you look around at those in ministry who have not gone through a process, then you can see their arrogance and the damage that they cause. It is almost always all about money. Sometimes you will see those in ministry who are bitter and judgmental, because they have unresolved pain and have been wounded and not yet healed. They are not yet done with their process and they leak their pain, anger and resentment onto everyone around them. When they speak, you do not hear the clear sound of heaven coming from them. Their process is not yet complete. They cannot see God's hand in what has been done to them.

Don't make your healing conditional on your vindication. If you wait to be vindicated, if you wait until revenge has been taken on those who hurt you, you need to go back into the "prison", because you are not yet ready. If you catch yourself thinking or fantasizing about vindication or revenge, then that is a sure sign you have not let go of some things and that you still need to forgive. When you see God's hand in your treatment by others, and you are focused on submitting to and rejoicing in Him, you know you are healed from your past. When you can release other people from guilt, and can even start providing for them as Joseph did, then you know God brought you there.

Development and training

After receiving a word or a promise, our character needs to be developed and we need to be trained in order to walk out that promise. During the time that Joseph was in Potiphar's house, and the time he was in prison, his character was developed, but not only that, he was trained. He received hands-on practical training that prepared him for his future in the palace. He developed skills that he would later need for the role he was to fulfill. During your time of development and training in your process, you can very easily fall into the trap of complaining and backsliding, and you are not aware that this is a major opportunity God is giving you to prepare for the future. Often people even walk away from God during this time, unaware of what He is doing and what He is preparing them for. Our "prison" never looks like the "palace" we will be working in later on.

During Joseph's time in Potiphar's home and in the prison, he learned the following things:

- He learned the language
- He learned about land management
- He learned about agriculture systems
- He learned about people management
- He learned how to work with very powerful people
- He learned about business
- He learned about government systems
- He learned political skills

When he initially received the dreams from God, he was a teenager with no life experience and no training in the subjects I just mentioned. Jacob and his sons led a nomadic life, tending to their flocks. How on earth would Joseph ever be capable of fulfilling the role that God showed him in a dream without some kind of training? Pharoah was a smart and well-educated man. He would not just allow an ex-convict who happened to interpret a dream to suddenly rule the land! No, I am sure that Joseph's achievements in prison and prior to that in Potiphar's home were communicated to Pharoah. Pharoah promoted Joseph because he saw that he was an excellent manager with a lot of experience, and could work in difficult circumstances and under stress. He had worked for one of the richest and most powerful men in the land, and had learned a new language. He also promoted Joseph because he could sense that God was with him and that he was filled with wisdom, but not arrogant. Joseph didn't claim to be able to interpret dreams, but humbly stated that it was God who gave him the interpretation.

Multiple tests

Joseph went through multiple tests. One of them was his purity. When Potiphar's wife tried to seduce him, and then angrily accused him of rape, his integrity was called into question. He could have said to himself, "With everything I have been through so far, being betrayed and sold as a slave, now living in the home of a wealthy and powerful man ... I am lonely and far from my family, but now I am successful and God is with me, and a beautiful woman wants me; why not?!" Instead, he said, "How then could I do such a wicked thing and sin against God?" (Gen 39:9). You need to decide ahead of time, before you are in that place of testing and temptation, what you will do. You need to choose not to sin before you are in the position to. Joseph ran from Potiphar's wife and sin, the only good thing to do.

He cannot sin against God, so he is thrown into prison accused of rape, and yet he did not do anything wrong. If he had thought he was in a bad place before, as a slave, he has now sunk even lower and is thrown in with the criminals.

He is seen as a slave who has betrayed his master. And everything he endured in the house of Potiphar was for nothing, or so he thought. Perhaps he thought that it was through his position in Potiphar's home that the prophetic dreams would be fulfilled. He was promised he would rule and reign, and it probably looked like that in Potiphar's home. He was the personal assistant to one of the most powerful men in Egypt. However, going from there to being the right-hand man of Pharoah is another thing altogether. When you are at the top of one mountain, you cannot jump to the next peak. You have to descend the mountain you are on, in order to climb the next one. You will enter into a whole new season of training and development as you climb the next mountain.

Joseph spent a long time in prison. He saw new prisoners come in and leave. He was stuck there. He could not promote himself. He could not make the prophecy come true. And even his own attempts at getting out of prison early failed miserably. In Genesis 40, we read that when the royal baker and Pharaoh's cupbearer were thrown into prison with Joseph, he successfully interpreted their dreams with God's help. He hoped that the cupbearer would put in a good word for him when he was released. And he knew he would be released because God had revealed that in the cupbearer's dream. Joseph was doing prison ministry, but from within. But oh, how he wanted to get out. However, it would take another two whole years before God's time came for Joseph to leave the prison. God's timing is always perfect, and if we try to speed things up, we can get ourselves into quite a mess. Or, in Joseph's case, have to wait for another two years.

Humility is key

Joseph was placed in several circumstances in which he had to learn humility. Humility is something we have to learn; it does not come naturally to us. Jesus was an example of humility for us. He humbled Himself and was born in a stable, as a fragile human baby. He knew his identity as the King of kings, and Lord of lords, and yet lived a simple life as the son of a carpenter. He did not draw attention to Himself and was not arrogant. He knew He was destined for greatness; He knew that He was the Promised One, the Savior of the world. There was no doubt in His mind of His calling and purpose here on earth. And yet, in all that, He was never proud. He had humble beginnings, lived a simple and humble life, and died the death of a criminal. Perhaps in your process you feel like a king in a stable. Or maybe not even like a king at all, in spite of the promise and calling on your life. King David was anointed by the prophet Samuel as king of all Israel, and then spent the greater part of the following years running for his life, hiding like a fugitive in caves and in the hills. I am sure David did not feel like he was king. All these three, Joseph, Jesus and David, learned humility, submitted themselves to God and His leadership, and all three were exalted in due time.

We too must learn humility, before we can ever be exalted by God. We can only rise up if we have been down low. Some of us find it hard to go down, difficult to humble ourselves. Some of us would have grabbed the opportunity to sleep with the boss' beautiful wife, or to throw ourselves from the top of the temple in the knowledge that God's angels would prevent us from dying, or killed Saul as he was relieving himself in the same cave we were hiding in. Some of us would have refused to stay in a stable because of our arrogance, and in that we would have missed the wise men carrying the provision and blessings.

[Jesus] Who, being in very nature God, did not consider equality with God something to be used to his own advantage; rather, he made himself nothing by taking the very nature of a servant, being made in human likeness. And being found in appearance as a man, he humbled himself by becoming obedient to death—even death on a cross! Therefore God exalted him to the highest place and gave

> him the name that is above every name, that at the name of Jesus
> every knee should bow, in heaven and on earth and under the earth,
> and every tongue acknowledge that Jesus Christ is Lord, to the glory
> of God the Father.
> – PHILIPPIANS 2:6-11

Is your pride blocking your blessing? Is it preventing you from learning much-needed lessons for your breakthrough? Can we be really honest about this? Is there a stubbornness in your character that is stopping you from getting through your process, from learning humility and growing in Christ-like character? Are you worried about what others will think? What will they say? Are you unwilling to spend time in "prison" because that cannot possibly be the path to the "palace"?

Spiritually we will look more like Jesus as we go through the seasons of life

---

Did you know that pride can be your prison? That it can stop you from walking in the promise and prophecy that God has given? Arrogance can create your own agony. It can prolong your time in the storm and the process. If the One whom we love and adore, worship and praise, was willing to be born in a stable, then why are we so arrogant that we are not willing to humble ourselves and be in a "stable" or in a "prison" (for doing what is right)? If we cannot learn humility, we cannot grow. If we cannot lower ourselves, we cannot be exalted. This may mean that we spend time as a "slave" or "do time" in a "prison".

The manifestation of the promise

The process that you have been through, the storm that you have survived, the prison time that you have served, will work out something in you that cannot be bought with money, that cannot be achieved with learning, that cannot be mimicked. It will make you authentic again. All of the things that were not nice have been removed, and the beauty of your character, the gifts and talents God placed inside of you, will be brought to the surface for you to shine. The seasons of the process have been completed; the manifestation of the promise is here. You will look back and see how much you have changed, what you have learned and how you have grown.

And when you have come through the storm and you are on the other side, you will realize that the lessons you learned can be passed on to others. You will recognize the process when it happens again in your life, perhaps in a different form, or when it happens in the life of another person. You will see that the depths of the next processes are less deep, the tests become easier to pass, because you have learned to lean on God and make Him the center of your life. Your character has been formed, you have matured, and though your promise has now been made manifest, when a new process comes it will not knock the breath out of you like the first time.

I am convinced that when you have learned well in your first cycle of seasons, the next seasons are easily recognizable and perhaps even easier to navigate. Your character is formed, you have ripened, you are experienced, you wrote history with God and now you can truly say, "I am a friend of God." Through all the seasons of testing and trials you learn and experience what it is like to go from a slave to being a son, and from being a son you grow into being a father for others, representing God the Father for the next generation.

Final thoughts

Dear friend, we are at the end of this book called *The Process*. Perhaps you just started your process, are in the middle of it, or almost at the end. Maybe you are in a self-inflicted storm, a demonic storm, a God storm, or maybe in the so-called perfect storm. Wherever you are in your process season and whichever storm you are facing, as you have read this book, my story, I hope that you have found things that bring clarification to your own process; that you will find encouragement to not give up when it feels all hope is lost, but to remain standing through the storm.

> God is with you and for you,
> and He will see you through

The storm will end. There will be a day when you look back on all that you have been through, and you will be able to say, "God is good. He was there with me when the waves came crashing into my life, when the storm blew and raged, and when I could no longer see where to go or what to do. It was Him who stood next to me and guided my steps, who held me tight, and whose Spirit spoke the truth of God's Word to my heart."

Remember, how you deal with the rejection you go through could be the test that shows you are able to deal with what God has for you in the next level, and that every time you are dealing with some sort of rejection, that this could be a sign that is pointing in God's direction for your life.

In this process you have learned or will learn that you will not discover the open door of your promise until you have dealt with the closed doors in your life. Remember, you are not your past and you are not going in that direction. You are not perfect but know that most parts of you are incredible and wonderfully made. You are originally made in God's own image. He is able to take everything that is broken, bruised and betrayed and make it whole, and use that for His glory.

Please know that you are not alone. Everyone who wants to be used by God will experience the story of being a harvest seed. A seed needs to be in the ground where it is dark, in order to produce fruit and harvest. Every hero of faith in the Bible but also our modern-day faith heroes have gone through a deep process before they walked in the fulfillment of their calling. What a privilege it is that you can join the army of faith heroes who went through it all, persevered till the end and conquered any storm and trial they faced.

Jesus said, I can take any situation, anything that looks completely paralyzed, and bring it to a brand-new place of restoration and transformation. God is with you and for you, and He will see you through. He has promised to never leave you nor forsake you (Heb. 13:5). When it feels like everyone has abandoned you, He has not and never will. May you know the peace that "transcends all understanding" (Phil. 4:7), even in the midst of the storm. Because when Jesus is in the boat, His command still stands.

> He got up, rebuked the wind and said to the waves, "Quiet! Be still!"
> Then the wind died down and it was completely calm.
> – MARK 4:39

Proclamations
of God's promises

I speak and confess God's word (Rom. 10:10).

Death and life are in the power of my tongue,
so I choose to speak life (Prov. 18:21).

I walk in the spirit of faith and I speak faith
(2 Cor. 4:13).

I move mountains by speaking in faith
(Mark 11:23).

What I declare will take place
(Isa. 45:21).

God has created me as spiritual being
with authority (Gen. 1:26-28).

I believe God's word, speak God's word and
receive his promises (Heb. 6:12).

I speak of the things that are not,
as if they already are (Rom. 4:17).

I stay out of trouble because I control
my tongue (Prov. 21:23).

My heart is good, I say good things and therefore
receive good things (Matt. 12:34-35).

I use the sword of the Spirit, God's Word (Eph. 6:17).

I bless others so that I will be blessed (1 Pet. 3:9).

I am a hero of faith, because I speak the blessing of God
(Heb. 11:20-21).

The Lord is my provider of everything
I need according to his riches in glory (Phil. 4:19).

The Lord is my righteousness
and He makes me holy. Through his sacrifice
I have been made holy and righteous (2 Cor. 5:21).

The Lord is my Shepherd,
I shall not want. He will lead me
to green pastures (Ps. 23).

The Lord is my victory and with God
I will overcome every obstacle (Jer. 1:19).

The Lord is my peace and I walk
in supernatural peace (John 14:27).

With God nothing is impossible in my life (Matt. 19:26).

My work is productive and fruitful (Deut. 30:9-10).

Everything I do will prosper (Ps. 1:3).

I will be prosperous and successful (Josh. 1:8).

I am blessed wherever I go (Deut. 28:6).

I am the head and not the tail,
I will go up and not down (Deut. 28:13).

God is my source and I will not experience
drought, because God's showers of blessings
have been poured out over me (Ps. 84:6).

I walk in obedience, listen to his voice,
and God has given me a place above all peoples
of the earth (Deut. 28:1).

All of God's blessings will come on me
and overtake me (Deut. 28:2).

I am blessed in the city and blessed
in the field. No matter where I am,
I am blessed (Deut. 28:3).

My descendants will be blessed (Gen. 12:1-7).

All enemies that attack me will be
defeated and will flee (Deut. 28:7).

God's blessing is on my finances (Prov. 10:22).

Everything I do, according to his will
and principals, will grow,
multiply and be blessed (Ps. 1:1-3).

All people will see that God is with me
and my family and that He has blessed us.
I will testify of his blessings (Deut. 28:1-14).

I will be blessed through the
storehouses of heaven, and there will always
be blessing and provision (Deut. 28:12).

I will lend and not borrow (Deut. 28:12).

Blessing and prosperity will be mine
and I will eat the fruit of my labor, because I fear God
and walk in obedience to Him (Ps. 128:1).

When I cry out to God in my distress
and He will answer me (Ps. 118:5).

I will live by faith. I do not doubt
but believe all of God's promises (Hab. 2:4).

I do what the Word of God says (James 1:22).

I will do all that Jesus did here on earth and even greater
things in faith and dependence on God (John 14:12).

I am not my past and I am looking
forward to the future (Phil. 3:13-14).

Wealth and riches are in my house and my
righteousness will endure forever (Ps. 112:3).

I am strong and powerful in the Lord (Eph. 6:10).

I am healed and free from every disease,
now and in the future. By his stripes
I have been healed. Sickness and disease have no
right to be in my body (Isa. 53:4-5, 1 Pet. 2:24).

Whatever comes out of my mouth is in line with God's word
and his promises (Prov. 18:21).

God has given me the keys to the kingdom
and everything that I bind on earth will be
bound in heaven (Matt. 16:19).

I have been given the nations as an inheritance and the
ends of the earth as my possession (Ps. 2:8).

My strength shall be renewed and I will soar
on eagle's wings (Isa. 40:31).

Jesus can calm every storm in my life as
He rules over the wind and the waves (Mark 4:39).

I am more than a conqueror in Jesus (Rom. 8:37).

Acknowledgments

I would like to dedicate this book with utmost gratitude and appreciation to the following individuals who have played significant roles in my journey:

First and foremost, I dedicate this book to my Lord Jesus Christ. His wisdom, power and boundless love have guided me through the most challenging and transformative phases of my life.

To my beloved wife and best friend, Laura: your unwavering love, support, prayers and wisdom have been instrumental in my journey. Your presence has been a source of strength, helping me navigate the process and restoring my heart. I am deeply grateful for you.

I also extend my heartfelt dedication to my beloved parents, whose unconditional love and patience have been my pillars of strength during the most trying times.

A special tribute goes to Pastor Bill Johnson, whose profound impact on my life deserves recognition. Through his guidance and Kingdom keys, I have learned to navigate the storms, celebrate God's goodness in all circumstances and remain focused on His presence and power. Your life and personal journey serve as an inspiration to me, as you embody the love and goodness of God in every situation.

Lastly, I want to express my sincere gratitude to my dear "twin" brother, Jean-Luc Trachsel. As one of my closest friends, you have walked with me through the valleys and continuously reminded me of God's calling upon my life.

May this book serve as a testimony to the faith, love and unwavering support I have received from these remarkable individuals.

About the author

Mattheus and Laura van der Steen are the founders and senior leaders of Harvest Fields International. Their desire is to see every person on earth having an authentic encounter with Jesus Christ through the power of the Holy Spirit.

Mattheus is a much sought-after speaker in churches, schools, conferences and evangelistic campaigns. His ministry is characterized by a straightforward proclamation of the gospel confirmed by the Holy Spirit with conviction, signs and wonders. His passion is to multiply and raise up a generation of revivalists, and to empower, equip and encourage the body of Christ to dream again and live a life of faith.

From the start, one of his guiding principles has been 'go where no one else goes'. This has led him to Myanmar, Laos, Russia, North Korea, Ukraine (during the war) and about eighty other countries. Wherever he goes, his aim is to bring together churches, networks and denominations for the sake of the harvest of souls. He is convinced that reaching everyone requires everyone.

Mattheus is part of leadership teams at Global Evangelist Alliance (GEA) and Asia Shall Be Saved (ASBS), and is board member of Europe Shall Be Saved (ESBS).

Mattheus and Laura are Dutch citizens who currently live in Florida, USA. They consider it a God-given privilege to live out His love as a family of six.

Harvest Fields International

harvestfieldsinternational.com

youtube.com/harvestfieldsinternational
facebook.com/harvestfieldsinternational
instagram.com/harvest_fields_international

Mattheus van der Steen

facebook.com/mattheusvandersteen
instagram.com/mattheusvandersteen

Online courses The Process

We would like to help you in the process you are going through.
Join our online courses for more in-depth teaching on the
different subjects discussed in *The Process*.

www.theprocess.courses

*Let's touch, reach, and impact
the nations together!*

Milton Keynes UK
Ingram Content Group UK Ltd.
UKHW021818121023
430461UK00015B/369

9 781960 678720